Physical Characteristics of the
Kuvasz

(from the American Kennel Club breed standard)

Back: Of medium length, straight, firm and quite broad.

Tail: Carried low, natural length reaching at least to the hocks. In repose it hangs down resting on the body, the end but slightly lifted.

Hindquarters: The portion behind the hip joint is moderately long, producing wide, long and strong muscles of the upper thigh. The femur is long, creating well-bent stifles. Lower thigh is long, dry, well muscled. Metatarsus is short, broad and of great strength.

Color: White. The skin is heavily pigmented. The more slate gray or black pigmentation the better.

Height: Measured at the withers: Dogs, 28 to 30 inches; bitches, 26 to 28 inches.

Weight: Dogs approximately 100 to 115 pounds; bitches approximately 70 to 90 pounds.

Coat: The Kuvasz has a double coat, formed by guard hair and fine undercoat. The texture of the coat is medium coarse. The coat ranges from quite wavy to straight.

Feet: Well padded. Pads resilient, black. Feet are closed tight, forming round "cat feet." Some hair between the toes, the less the better. Dark nails are preferred. Feet as in front, except the rear paws somewhat longer.

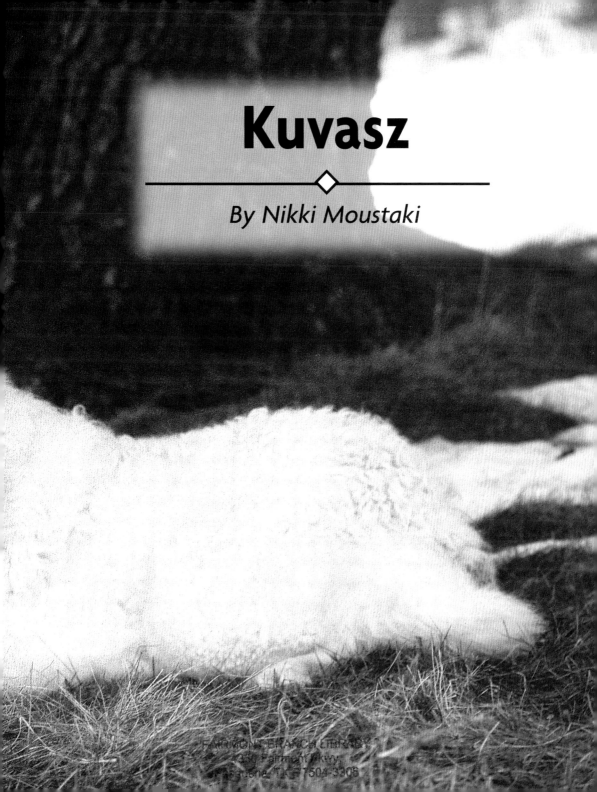

Kuvasz

◇

By Nikki Moustaki

Contents

KENNEL CLUB BOOKS® **KUVASZ**
ISBN: 1-59378-381-7

Copyright © 2007 • Kennel Club Books, LLC • 308 Main Street, Allenhurst, NJ 07711 USA
Cover Design Patented: US 6,435,559 B2 • Printed in South Korea

Library of Congress Cataloging-in-Publication Data
Moustaki, Nikki, 1970-
Kuvasz / by Nikki Moustaki.
    p. cm.
  ISBN 1-59378-381-7
1. Kuvasz. I. Title.
SF429.K88M68 2006
636.73--dc22
                                2006011615

        10 9 8 7 6 5 4 3 2 1

Photography by Isabelle Français and Lara Stern
with additional photos by:

Kim Booth, Paulette Braun, Alan and Sandy Carey, Carolina Biological Supply, Carol Ann Johnson, Bill Jonas, Dr. Dennis Kunkel, Tam C. Nguyen, Phototake, Jean Claude Revy, Chuck Tatham and Alice van Kempen.

Illustrations by Patricia Peters.

The publisher wishes to thank all of the owners whose dogs are illustrated in this book.

The Publisher dedicates this book
to a great friend and dog man
Greg Warne (1950-2006),
whose love of the Kuvasz breed
and his friends, family and associates at
BowTie, Inc. remains with all of us forever.

HISTORY OF THE

KUVASZ

The modern Kuvasz has its direct roots in Hungary, but this breed has a rich and ancient history. The Kuvasz is perhaps one of the oldest breeds in the world, an ancestor to dozens of other breeds and recorded in the histories of several countries over thousands of years. Throughout its history, the Kuvasz has always served as a guard and herding dog.

Archeologists estimate that the history of the Kuvasz begins sometime around 6600 BC in the Tigris-Euphrates Valley, the area that is now Iraq and its neighboring countries. The ancient Kuvasz worked on trade routes between Europe and Asia, generally accompanying nomads and their flocks. As a result of this constant movement, the ancient Kuvasz probably bred with other kinds of dog common at the time. Many other breeds are thought to have their beginnings with the Kuvasz; for example, the Tibetan Mastiff, Great Pyrenees, Samoyed, Maremma Sheepdog, Anatolian Shepherd (Karabash), Akbash Dog, Tatra Sheepdog, Slovac Cuvac and Shar Planinetz. The two closest relatives of the Kuvasz, though, are the Komondor and the Puli, two other native breeds of Hungary.

The name Kuvasz originates from *Kuassa*, a Sumerian word originating over 7,000 years ago. *Ku* meant "dog" and *Assa* meant

Belonging to the family of large white flock guardians, the Hungarian Komondor is one of the closest relatives of the Kuvasz.

"horse," combining to describe this animal as a "horse dog," an early reflection of the way that the Kuvasz worked on farms to protect the horses and livestock. Other theories about the origins of the breed place it in Russia and have it named after the Chuvash people, who kept this dog to guard over their livestock. Written records of the Kuvasz go back to Mesopotamia around 5000 BC in the city of Ugarit. While exploring the ruins of this city in 1931, Sir H. J. McDonald found a clay tablet with the dog's name inscribed on it in cuneiform (one of the earliest writing systems). Kuvaszok were also included on clay tablets uncovered in what was formerly the city of Ur. These tablets are presumably from around 3500 BC.

Perhaps the most famous ancient mention of the Kuvasz is in the Code of Hammurabi. This text describes a system of laws and was written by King Hammurabi around 1780 BC. The Kuvasz is actually referred to by its modern name in this text. It is amazing to think that the breed has retained the same title and purpose for thousands of years. The durability of this breed is further proof of its success as a working dog.

Around 900 AD, a tribe called the Magyars invaded the Carpathian Basin, taking over the land now known as Hungary. They brought dogs with them,

which bred with the native dogs like the Kuvasz. Influences such as this certainly affected the breed. By 1443, the Kuvasz was quite popular, eventually becoming a favorite of the king of Hungary, Matthias Corvinus. The breed was the preferred guard and hunting companion of the powerful nobility during this time and was not found in the homes of the poor. The king established a careful breeding program to produce better Kuvaszok. He preferred them over human guards and kept the dogs by his side at all times. He also gave the dogs as gifts. One of the people said to have been awarded one of these special dogs was Count Dracula (Vlad the Impaler) on the occasion of his marriage to the king's daughter after his release from the king's prison.

Eventually, this area was taken over by the Ottoman-Turkish Empire. During this time, the dog's common name, Kuassa, was changed to Kawasz, meaning "nobility's armed guard." With King Matthias Corvinus gone, the Kuvasz soon returned to its life on the farm, where its abilities were best served. Even today, the name Kuvasz means "café-keeper" in Turkish. For several more centuries, the Kuvasz worked primarily guarding horses, sheep and other livestock on farms.

The Hungarian Kennel Club was formed in 1880. The first

official standard for the Kuvasz, which only emphasized its performance ability, was approved five years later. In 1883 the first Kuvasz competed in a conformation show. Two Kuvaszok were brought to a show in Vienna by Count d'Esterházy. Two years later, the first breed standard was written for the Kuvasz in Hungary. This was certainly many years in the making, but the Kuvasz earned its official place in both the field and the show ring.

In 1912 the standard was revised to more clearly define breed characteristics and this resulted in improved breed uniformity. Consequently, world interest increased and the Kuvasz began to be exported to Germany, Holland, Switzerland and the United States.

THE KUVASZ IN THE UNITED STATES
By Connie Townsend and Bea Page

The first Kuvaszok in the United States were brought across the ocean in 1920 as the pets of an immigrant Hungarian couple. The couple was eventually forced to part with their dogs for financial reasons, and their male dog found a new home with Miss Mabel Marsh (to become Mrs. J. Scoffield Rowe) from New Jersey in the late 1920s. Miss Marsh took more than the average interest in her then-unusual dog and worked tirelessly

A noble breed indeed, the Kuvasz was once popular among Hungarian royalty.

to bring a female Kuvasz from Hungary as a mate for him. With this pair, she became the first person in the United States to breed the Kuvasz, and she established the Romance kennels in the early 1930s.

The kennel only lasted until the late 1930s but accomplished much in its short time of operation. In 1931, Miss Marsh had the first Kuvasz admitted into the American Kennel Club's (AKC) stud book. Aino Andres, a long-time Kuvasz fancier, reported in two *Dog World* articles, November and December of 1978, that the first Kuvasz was registered with the American Kennel Club in August 1931. The entry is listed as follows: "Tamar v. Wurmtal, Bitch (791,292) Owner Ignatz Schmidt. Breeder Rudolf Fischer, Germany. Whelped Dec. 16, 1925. White, black nose. By Sultan von Rosenhain out of Dumm von Franken." Miss Andres went on to say that, "Both Sultan and Dumm came from a mixed bag of

Hungarian and German dogs, most of them simple farm dogs, but pure-bred and registered."

Tamar v. Wurmtal was bred to a Hungarian male in Los Angeles and produced a male puppy in July 1928, Rigoletto von Romance. The sire, Futykos von Cibakhaza, was never AKC registered. Miss Mabel E. Marsh was the owner of Rigoletto, and he was the first to bear the Romance kennel name.

Miss Marsh was able to get the dam, Tamar, registered with the AKC, and in 1934 Rigoletto was registered. At that time she also registered an imported Hungarian female, Csiba-Te.

At one time, Kuvaszok were held in such high regard that they were only to be owned by the upper tiers of society.

FROM FIELD TO FAMILY
The Kuvasz is an ancient Hungarian herding dog. Eventually, it was taken from the field and treasured by nobility as a fierce guard dog. The breed eventually found its way back into the field to do its original job of protecting livestock. It has recently moved into a more urban setting, where the breed is now prized as a family guardian and companion.

Csiba-Te whelped her first litter of four, sired by Rigoletto, on February 6, 1932.

Miss Andres reported that through the 1930s Miss Marsh campaigned aggressively to gain the American Kennel Club's recognition of the Kuvasz. Under the kennel name Romance, she bred, imported, exhibited and advertised in the New York/New Jersey area. The first four AKC Kuvasz champions were Ch. Gilda of Romance, Ch. Astor von Ostseestrand, Ch. White Knight of Romance and Ch. Rigoletto of Romance II.

Miss March imported Astor von Ostseestrand, a five-year-old German champion, who sired four litters of puppies. In 1936 she imported two Hungarian Kuvaszok, a male and a female, from Count Uchtritz-Amade. The male was never bred. The female, Lokosi Bajos, produced litters in 1938 and in 1939. Miss

March also imported Almo v. Arabienhof, a male, from Switzerland in 1936. He sired three litters, the last in 1940.

In 1935 she entered her American-bred Kuvasz in the Westminster Kennel Club Dog Show and showed it in the regular class, as well as in the team and brace competitions. That same year the AKC approved the official standard for the breed in the United States, which remained in place until 1974. Her last litter was recorded in December of 1940. After only 8 years, at least 17 litters and at least 5 imported dogs, Romance kennels was no longer active.

In the late 1930s, Miss Marsh married J. Scoffield Rowe; her husband's untimely death in 1940

WWII

Bitter wars in Europe separated Kuvasz owners in various countries, and bloodlines became diluted as breeders tried to correct "faults" in the breed. For example, it is suspected that the Germans introduced the Great Pyrenees into their Kuvasz stock to straighten its coat, though this isn't proven and may be simply anecdotal. Some people believe that after World War II Hungarians bred their dogs with the German type, resulting in dogs that did not appear very much like the written standard.

essentially caused the end of the kennel, and many of the dogs were sold. A few Romance dogs were bred by their owners in the 1940s but only one, Sir Christopher of Fresno, sired a litter as late as 1950.

By World War II, the Kuvasz was still popular in Europe, used as both a livestock dog and a police dog. Unfortunately, the breed did such a good job protecting its villages that it was targeted by invading armies. Others were shot by their owners so that they wouldn't give up their hiding places. The dogs that weren't killed outright starved to death. These factors, along with limited financial resources after

Following the Ottoman-Turkish takeover, Kuvaszok returned to the field as guards of livestock.

the war and no one focusing on breeding, caused the Kuvasz to become nearly extinct after the war, with fewer than 30 individuals of the breed remaining.

When the war ended, many factory workers wanted Kuvaszok to guard their properties, but there were few to be found. In Hungary, the breed's native country, only 12 individual dogs remained. Nearly every remaining Kuvasz was gathered from across Europe, and a breeding program was instituted. The breed's numbers began increasing again.

The first Kuvasz club began in the US in 1939. There were still not many of the dogs in the country, but much effort was being put into increasing their numbers. It was also during the mid to late 1930s that Kuvaszok began to appear at dog shows. Around this time, another couple came to the aid of the Kuvasz: Mr. and Mrs. Ziegler of Manchester, Pennsylvania. The couple brought over a German dog, Dickens Von Leonardshof. They were so dedicated to making the Kuvasz more common in America that they persevered in spite of financial difficulties. The couple imported another dog, Rike Von Waldfrid, and the pair of Kuvaszok produced ten puppies.

These Kuvasz puppies were shown at the Morris and Essex show in New Jersey as well as at the Westminster Kennel Club show at Madison Square Garden. The Zieglers did much for the Kuvasz as a breed in just a few short years, but they were ultimately forced to stop breeding dogs as they got older.

For the next decade or so, the Kuvasz remained very much in the background of the American dog world. No one was working to produce quality Kuvaszok in the country, and therefore the breed's numbers did not increase much. The occasional litter was born, but breeding was very infrequent.

Despite the scarcity of breeding stock, two American kennels, Mrs. Margaret Hutchinson of Wish-A-Way and

Historically bred to be the guardian of the flock, the Kuvasz also assumes the post of companion and show dog.

Though primarily a guardian of stock, some Kuvaszok have demonstrated a knack at herding their keep as well.

Mr. and Mrs. N. De Lorenzo of Oznerol, promoted the breed in the 1950s. From 1940 to 1966, only five Kuvasz earned their AKC championships: Ch. Rike v Waldfried, Ch. Anitra von Premer, Ch. Wish-A-Way's Hassan von Elfin, Ch. Condor Oznerol and Ch. Gyapjus Kapitany. Also during this period, the first obedience Companion Dog titles were awarded to Kuvasz; the recipients were Anika From The Farm CD and Amigo von Premer CD.

In the mid 1960s Dana Alvi became an active breeder and advocate for the Kuvasz. Her foundation bitch, Mex. Ch. Tall Grass Princess Magda, was imported from Canada. Magda was bred to Ch. Gyapjus Kapitany in April 1966 and then to Moby Dick in November 1966. From these litters, she crossbred offspring. In 1969, she used a male Hungarian import, Nagyhazi Betyar, to strengthen her lines.

The first *Kuvasz Newsletter* was printed in January 1966. This periodical attracted Kuvasz owners interested in increasing the quality and popularity of the breed. These people worked together to breed the Kuvasz more regularly, and the number of Kuvaszok in the United States continued to grow.

On April 30, 1966 a small group of Kuvasz fanciers formed the Kuvasz Club of America (KCA) under the leadership of Dana Alvi. The purpose of the club was to encourage and promote the breeding of quality Kuvaszok, to educate and guide novice owners and to share experiences and ideas among breeders. It wasn't until 1986 that the Kuvasz Club of America was incorporated.

The preliminary constitution that was adopted by the KCA was received from the American Kennel Club. The Kuvasz Club of America accepted this constitution with only one addition—the

While not as popular as other breeds, the Kuvasz is headed for a bright future as enthusiasts continue to promote the breed.

and Dana Alvi, became the first Kuvasz in the US to receive the Best in Show honor at the Starved Rock Kennel Club show in Ottawa, Illinois. Odin's show career included a total of 25 Group placements: 3 Fours, 7 Threes, 9 Twos, 5 Ones and the much coveted Best in Show.

Other Kuvasz kennels active during the '60s and '70s were Hugh and Luciana Glasgow of Glasgow and Clifford and Shirley Rutter of Pridonis. The 1970s and 1980s saw the following new breeders appear to carry on in the preservation of the breed: Ethel Adams of E'Don kennels, Sally Furgeson of Santa's Forest, Claudia Buss of Aquilon, Aino Andres and Doris Bartels of Budavari, Loretta Ouellette of Whiteacres/Whitewoods and Nancy McGuire of Oak Hill. Today, Sally Furgeson and Bonnie Leech are still breeding Kuvasz under the Santa's Forest kennels name.

In the 1960s and 1970s, there were so few Kuvaszok being shown that the breed qualified for the "Sexes Combined" class. That meant that a single male and a single female entry combined constituted one point for the winner. From 1936 through 1969, 17 Kuvasz championships and 2 Companion Dog titles were earned, although from 1959 through 1965 no Kuvasz earned an AKC title. As the breed

recommendation that Kuvasz owners x-ray their dogs. The following is a quote from a letter sent to the KCA membership by Dana Alvi: "The part in the constitution, to urge Kuvasz owners to x-ray their dogs was placed there at my suggestion. We are rather proud that the AKC accepted this section and believe that our club was the only one in the United States at the time to have this concern mentioned in its constitution."

Between 1968 and 1979, 33 Champions, 7 Companion Dogs and 1 Companion Dog Excellent were AKC titled under the Hamralvi kennels name. On July 10, 1977, Ch. Hamralvi Heimdall Odin (Odin), handled by Doug McClain for owners Lynn Schiesel

gained popularity from 1970 through 1986, however, the AKC recorded titles for 214 Champions, 48 Companion Dogs, 8 Companion Dog Excellents and 1 Tracking Dog.

At the first Sanctioned "B" Match, held on August 26, 1972 in Columbus, Ohio, Best in Match was Hamralvi Jeges Medve Indas. On May 29, 1973 the KCA supported the Queensboro Kennel Club (New York) with a record entry of 17 Kuvaszok. The Best of Breed winner was Ch. Devilo Prince Khan. Khan went on to a fourth place in the Working Group to become the first male Kuvasz to get a Group placement. The first

female Kuvasz to win a Group placement was Ch. Hamralvi Own That Girl on March 24, 1974. She was owned by Claudia Buss of Aquilon kennels. The first Companion Dog Excellent title was earned in 1979 by Ch. Danlos Pericle CDX.

Prior to this time little attention was paid to hip dysplasia. As the Kuvasz Club of America and Kuvasz breeders educated owners and new breeders, the Orthopedic Foundation for Animals' (OFA) listing for clear hips started to grow. By the early 1980s, there were 82 cleared Kuvaszok listed with OFA. The first was Kyomi

Known for its hard work and durability, the Kuvasz is a fantastic breed for many outdoor activities.

May Casewe, and the second was Tall Grass Gay Liesel.

In 1982 Elizabeth Kondor (Pyramid kennels) obtained a Hungarian import from Miss Kinga Fabo of Calgary, named Can. Ch. Budagyongye Opal (Opal), who won a Canadian Best in Show in 1977. He earned his AKC championship in August 1982. Both his sire and dam were well-recognized Hungarian champions. He became a significant addition to the American Kuvasz gene pool, siring 28 champions. Opal can be found in the extended pedigree of most of the Best in Show-winning Kuvasz today.

Am./Can./Int./Puerto Rican/South Am. Ch. Oak Hill's Captain Courageous ITT (Captain), bred by Marla Adams and Nancy McGuire and owned by Nancy McGuire and Darla Lofranco, had a significant impact on the breed. A descendant of the first BIS winner, Odin, Captain became a champion in 1984. He was the first Kuvasz to receive an International Temperament Test Certificate. He sired 13 champions. He is also found in the extended pedigree of some Best in Show winners.

It wasn't until November 27, 1987 that the second Best in Show in United States Kuvasz history was awarded, and it went to Ch.

Here's a very well-traveled Kuvasz, Am./Can./Int./Puerto Rican/South Am. Ch. Oak Hill's Captain Courageous ITT.

Am./Can. Ch. Oak Hill's Inanna of Sumer takes a Best in Specialty under judge Michelle Billings.

Santa's Forest Title Wave (Soka), bred and owned by Sally Furgeson. An Opal descendant, he sired five champion get. He is also a descendant of Am./Can. Ch. Santa's Forest Danielle, who produced 12 champions, 9 of which were sired by Opal.

In 1987 the first AKC tracking title was awarded to a Kuvasz, Dahmer's Ursa Minor Minnie TD, owned by Richard and Kathleen Dahmer. It wasn't until 1990 that the second tracking title was awarded, and it went to Lofranco's Impero Joshua CD, TD, also owned by the Dahmers.

The late '80s and '90s saw further growth with the addition of a number of new kennels: Valerie and Gary Eastman of Ghosthill, Sue Thomas of Mauna Kea, Agi and Sandor Hejja of Starhaven, Fred and Gudrun Stein of Bjel-Saros, Marla Adams of Damara Magyar/later Marla and Dave Conkey of Telperion, Herbert Sweeny of Macsuibhne, Dr. Henry and Karen Nichols of Nordland, Bobbie Kelley of August, Lorraine and William Blosser of Walors, Henry and Millie Fellerman of

Rocky Mountain High, Linda Lloyd of Czigany, Susan Secor of Gwyndura, Dawn and Randy Ham of Peachtree, Lynn Brady and Connie Townsend of Szumeria, Chuck and Kathy Ringering of Double Ring and Debbie Blank of Glacier Creek.

In 1989 the first Utility Dog title was achieved by Ch. Glasgow's Avalanche Aerro UD, owned by Dr. Connie Petrick.

In July of 1992, Am./Can. Ch. Oak Hill's Inanna of Sumer (Inanna), bred by Nancy McGuire and Janet Kleber and owned by Lynn Brady and Connie Townsend, began her show career.

At 18 months, she was 1992's top Kuvasz of the year with over 20 Group placements in 4 months. On December 6, 1992 she won Best in Show in Brantford, Canada.

Also in 1992, two handsome male Kuvaszok were coming to the attention of judges and the breed fanciers. Ch. Nordland's Rocky (Rocky), bred and owned by Dr. Henry and Karen Nichols, gained his championship at age 18 months and began placing in the Group. Am./Mex./Int. Ch. Szatmari Shadow of The Chief (Shadow), bred by Paul Yuhas of Budapest and owned by David

Ch. Szumeria's Same Old Song or "Ditto" winning Best of Opposite Sex in 1998.

and Marla Conkey, was beginning to take some Group placements as well.

After fulfilling the AKC's requirements, the KCA formally became a member club and the parent club for Kuvasz in September of 1992. The first national specialty was held on June 4, 1993 in Reno, Nevada, with an entry of 100 in conformation, 21 in sweepstakes and 8 in obedience. Conformation classes were judged by Mr. Robert H. Ward and the sweepstakes classes were judged by Dana Alvi of Hamralvi kennels. Best of Breed was Ch. Czigany Abracadabra, bred, owned and handled by Linda Lloyd, who later became an AKC judge. Ch. Szatmari Shadow of The Chief won an Award of Merit. Ms. Alvi's Best in Sweeps and Reserve Winners Bitch went to a nine-month-old female, Szumeria's Arsenic and Old Lace, bred by Lynn Brady and Connie Townsend and owned by Doreen MacPherson. Best of Opposite Sex in Sweeps went to her litter brother Szumeria's Affordable Luxury, owned by Jenny Chua and Dennis Soong. They were out of Ch. Oak Hill's Goin For The Gold by Ch. Oak Hill's I'm Mr. Rock 'N Roll (an Inanna littermate).

Inanna, Rocky and Shadow competed heavily for the remainder of 1993. Shadow sired a litter out of Ch. Telperions Thanksgiving Day which produced two beautiful bitches, Telperion Halima ("Bean"), owned by David and Marla Conkey, and Telperion Himalay, owned by David and Suzanne Wille.

The year 1993 culminated with Inanna's being awarded the first Best in Show for a female Kuvasz in the US on November 28, 1993 at Greater Naples Dog Club under judge Eleanor Evers. In July of 1993, Inanna became the top-winning Kuvasz of all time with over 11 Group Ones, 10 Group Twos, 18 Group Threes, 10 Group Fours and 117 Bests of Breed. She was the number 1 Kuvasz in breed and all-breed and the number 15 working dog. She ended the year with a Group One win at the Western Reserve Kennel Club in Cleveland, Ohio with an entry of over 850 working dogs.

The second KCA national specialty was held in 1994 in Louisville, Kentucky. Inanna, Rocky and Shadow were in this competition. Mrs. Michele Billings awarded Best of Breed to Inanna, Best of Opposite Sex to Shadow (who died of torsion shortly after in July) and an Award of Merit to Rocky. Winners Bitch and Best of Winners was Shadow's daughter, Telperion Halima (Bean). Two additional females were honored with Awards of Merit. The first was Ch. Mauna Kea's Promises To Keep, bred by Sue Thomas and owned by Sue Thomas and Sue McCarthy. She was a daughter of Rocky's sire. The second was Ch. Aquilon Photo Finish, bred by Claudia Buss and owned by Linda Harvey.

Inanna was retired in 1994 and was bred to Rocky by frozen semen implant. A single pup resulted, Szumeria's Sumer Solo (Sumer). She became an American and Canadian champion, multiple Group winner and Best of Breed winner at the Westminster Kennel Club show in 1997. Both Inanna and Rocky carry the genes of Best in Show-winners Opal and Odin in their pedigree. Inanna is also descended from Captain.

Rocky had by now matured into quite a showman and hit his stride in the conformation ring with his breeder/owner/handler Dr. Henry Nichols. On May 28, 1994 Rocky became the fourth Kuvasz to win a KCA Best in Show at the Spokane Kennel Club under judge Judy Doniere and the first breeder/owner-handled Kuvasz to win a Best in Show. He won a second Best in Show in the fall at the Whidbey Island Kennel Club in Washington state under judge Dr. Robert Indeglia on November 20, 1994. He was now the breed's only multiple Best in Show winner. He was bred to Am./Int./Mex. Ch. Nobility Southampton Bella ITT, bred by Kim and Kevin Carlson and owned by Jeannette Chiappero.

On other fronts, 1994 brought the start of the AKC Canine Good Citizen® (CGC) Program. The first Kuvasz to be certified was Ch. Asgard-Lofranco I Want It All. Many Kuvaszok have since received the CGC certification. The year 1994 also saw 71 new Kuvaszok OFA hip clearances, 6 OFA elbow clearances and 1 OFA patella clearance. Unfortunately, only 43% of the 89 AKC stud book entrants for 1994 had clearances for hips. The number of elbow clearances was even less. The majority of those dogs without hip clearances were owned by people who were not members of the KCA. The KCA breeders list has since grown to a current sixteen member breeders.

The third national specialty was held in Los Angeles, California on May 5, 1995 with an entry of 82 in conformation, 23 in sweepstakes and 11 in obedience. Best of Breed was awarded to Inanna and Best of Opposite Sex was awarded to Rocky.

Competition was strong in 1995. Mr. Robert Ward, the judge from the first national specialty, awarded Ch. Telperion Halima (Bean) a Best in Show at Abilene Kennel Club in Texas on January 28, 1995. On the West Coast, Ch. Ederra's Canis Major Arrakis (Major), owned by Maria Arechaederra, began to excel in the show ring, as did Ch.

Four-time Best in Show winner Ch. Nordland's Rocky getting number two.

Telperion Himalay (Sacha). Like her sister Bean, Sacha was awarded a Best in Show. In Colorado, Ch. Rocky Mountain High Avalanche, bred and owned by Millie and Hank Fellerman, was making his mark. In the East, Ch. Lofranco's Autumn Tirza, bred by Darla Lofranco and owned by Steve and Alice Kovacs, was making a mark. In Alaska there was Ch. Glacier Creek's Artic Thunder and Ch. Brantwood's Artic Adventure, both owned by Debbie Blank and Kenneth Butters. In the South there was Ch. Mission's Brut Pezsgo Kiadas (Bubbles), bred by Nancy Schefcick and owned by Lynn and Bruce Vogel.

Rocky racked up two more Bests in Show, for a total of four, and took the title of top-winning Kuvasz in breed history from

Inanna. Inanna and Rocky were bred a second time, producing Ch. Szumeria's Nala of Silverpick (Nala), Ch. Szumeria's Fertile Crescent and Ch. Szumeria's Sargon of Sumer. Nala would go on to win three national specialties and six all-breed Bests in Show, thereby taking the title of top-winning Kuvasz in breed history from her sire. Her record remains unbroken today.

At nine months of age, Nala was a multiple Group placer and won Best of Breed during the 1996 national specialty weekend, finishing her championship from the Bred-by-Exhibitor Class. This win was over an entry of 85 Kuvaszok, including the previous day's national specialty winner, Ch. Telperion Himalay, as well as Ch. Telperion Halima, Group-winning Ch. Ederra's Canis Major Arrakis and Nala's dam Ch. Oak Hill's Inanna of Sumer. The judge at that show was Les Benis, a longtime Puli breeder, who co-authored the first book on the Kuvasz with Dana Alvi. Nala was always breeder/owner-handled by Lynn Brady, who had never campaigned a dog prior to showing Nala.

Inanna and Rocky were bred for the third and last time in November 1996 and had three pups: Ch. Szumeria's Mr. Rock N' Roll, Ch. Szumeria's Same Old Song and Szumeria's Maggie Mae, bringing their total to seven puppies. All seven pups produced by this pair had OFA clear hips with multiple other OFA clearances.

On October 26, 1996 Nala received her first Best in Show at 16 months of age under judge Mr. Norm Herbel. Mr. Herbel had a history with the breed. He was the sweepstakes judge at the third KCA national specialty in California. Nala ended 1996 as the number-one Kuvasz at age 18 months. Some other top contenders showing during this same time were Ch. Ederra's Canis Major Arrakis (Major), owned by Maria Arechaedderra; Ch. Dejavu's Somethin 'T' Talk About, bred/ owned by Patricia Kemberling, MD; and Ch. Mauna Kea's Heart's Afire ("Markie"), bred and owned by Sue Thomas.

In the '90s, the AKC added the sport of agility to its competition. Kuvasz owners rose to the challenge of obtaining titles in this new sport, with Ch. Asgard-Lofranco I Want It All CD, TD, NA being the first to achieve a Novice Agility title on April 28, 1996.

Nineteen ninety-seven saw 43 new champions finished, 64 OFA hip clearances, 18 OFA elbow clearances, 2 OFA thyroid clearances and 19 Canine Eye Registry Foundation (CERF) eye clearances. Also reported were three Institute of Genetic Disease Control (GDC) hip clearances. In 1998 the first OFA Cardiac

Brood Bitch
winner Am./Can.
Ch. Oak Hill's
Inanna of Sumer
with Nala and
Ditto.

clearance was published. The vast improvement in health clearances can be credited to the educational programs and encouragement of the KCA.

It was also in 1997 that the first Kuvasz health study was prepared and sent to KCA members. Results were published in the KCA's newsletter, the *Kuvasz Quarterly*. The KCA also developed a website: www.kuvasz.com. The website improved communication with the membership and enhanced public education in the breed.

Unfortunately, a rift in the club came about around this time over the change in the breed standard to remove the disqualifi-

cation for "any color other than white," which resulted in the loss of many valuable members. Sue Thomas, as chair of the KCA Judges Education Committee, worked to contract new drawings for the Judges' Education Council, in conjunction with the Breed Standard Committee. The revised information was presented in articles for member review in the *Kuvasz Quarterly*.

At the 1997 national specialty, Nala was awarded Best of Breed under Judge Ms. Patricia Webster Laurans. Inanna was awarded the Brood Bitch Class, with Nala and River shown as her get. In 1998 and 1999, Nala won her third and fourth national specialty Bests of

Breed. Best of Opposite Sex at these nationals was her brother, Ch. Szumeria's Same Old Song ("Ditto"). Nala's dam, Inanna, was again Best Brood Bitch at these two nationals. An Award of Merit was awarded at the 1999 national to Ch. Mauna Kea's Heart's Afire ("Markie") and Ch. Augustove Holiday Hope. Markie's daughter, Mauna-Ederra's Double Image, out of Major, was awarded Winners Bitch.

Rocky Mountain Summer Jazz (Kenai), who would become a star in performance events, was getting his career underway. On September 5, 1998 he completed his Companion Dog title. On the same day he completed his Novice Agility title with a first place finish. On September 7, he earned his first leg in Novice Jumpers with Weaves agility with a second place. He was bred by Millie Fellerman and is owned, trained and handled by Barb Behan.

A Nala granddaughter, Ch. Szumeria's Wildwood Ruby Tuesday earns a Group One at the Anderson Kennel Club in 2004.

A prestigious Best of Breed at Westminster and a Group Four under Judge Lynette Saltzman targeted Markie for the attention of judges. She won back-to-back Bests in Show on April 10 and 11, 1999 under Lynette Saltzman and Richard Bauer. On June 6, her third Best In Show was awarded by Kenneth Buxton. Markie was handled by Mary and Brian Clegg. Also shown successfully that year was Florence Mattice's Nordland-Nobility Virginia C, a Rocky daughter. In the performance rings, Kenai continued to rack up titles, becoming the first Kuvasz to qualify at the Open level in agility.

Markie's daughter, Ch. Mauna-Ederra's Double Image (Image), followed in her dam's footsteps as a Westminster Best of Breed winner and Group placer, who at a later all-breed show became the ninth AKC Best in Show-winning Kuvasz. The BIS title was awarded by judge Ms. Charlotte Clem McGowan, who had given Image Winners Bitch at the 1999 national. Other specials in the breed ring were Ch. Santa's Forest Silver King and Ch. Double Ring Kastaspell.

Another budding performance star showed up on the horizon about this time. Ch. Szumeria's Legend NA (Legend), an Inanna and Rocky descendant bred to bring in the genes of BIS Ch. Santa's Forest Title Wave, began his career with a first place in Novice Agility.

Competition was stiff at the 2000 national specialty, but surprisingly a young bitch who was moved up from the classes, after completing her championship the previous weekend, was awarded Best In Specialty Show, and hence, Ch. Szumeria's Flying First Class ("Delta") became the third generation Szumeria dog to achieve a BISS. Delta was an Inanna and Rocky descendant, sired by Ch. Szumeria's Same Old Song ("Ditto") out of Ch. Szumeria's Shamont Select. Best of Opposite Sex and Best Veteran went to Rocky. Nala and Image received Awards of Merit. Winners Dog, Best of Winners and Best Puppy was Szumeria's Jamaican Music ("Marley"), who was out of a repeat breeding which produced Delta. Marley was only six months old. In 2003 he would win Best of Opposite Sex at the national and Best of Breed on the two days following the national. He would become the fifth dog in breed history to qualify for the KCA's highest conformation award. Winners Bitch and Best Bred By Exhibitor was Szumeria's Queen of Hearts, and High In Trial was Szumeria's Starlight Express, owned by Doreen MacPherson. These wonderful accomplishments demonstrate the success of Inanna x Rocky descendants.

Image continued her winning ways in 2001, going Best in Specialty Show. Her dam, Markie, was Best Brood Bitch and Best Veteran (and two years later Markie would come from the Veteran Class to win the 2003 national specialty). Awards of Merits for 2001 went to Ch. Szumeria's Flying First Class ("Delta") and Ch. Glacier Creek's Artic Spirit ("Sonia"). Sonia had a long and successful show career before her early demise from bloat, including a BIS in January of 2003. Ch. Rocky Mtn Whale Of A Deal ("Jonah"), who would go on to be the 2002 Best In Specialty Show winner, was Best Stud Dog at the 2001 national. By the end of the year, Image had 5 Bests in Show, was the number-1 Kuvasz in breed and all-breed and the number-13 Working dog. Double Ring kennels ended the year with three dogs in the top five, Ch. Double Ring Kastaspell, Ch. Double Ring Moonlight Serenade and Ch. Double Ring Butiful Dreamer.

Also in 2001, a very important program was announced by the AKC Canine Health Foundation and the Orthopedic Foundation for Animals. The Canine Health Information Center (CHIC) program was developed to provide a source of health information for owners, breeders and scientists that would assist in breeding healthy dogs. The Kuvasz Club of America was one of the first breed parent clubs to identify specific criteria for inclusion in the CHIC program. The club specified hip, elbow and thyroid testing for a Kuvasz to receive a CHIC number. The information is kept on an open database on the web, easily accessible to breeders and the general public.

A number of very nice dogs could be found at show rings across the country in 2001: Ch. Mattiaci Stratus Symbol (Stratus), a Rocky descendant; 2002's Best in Specialty Show winner, Ch. Rocky Mtn Whale Of A Deal (Jonah); Ch. Szumeria's Wildwood Ruby Tuesday (Tuesday), a Nala granddaughter; and Ch. Szumeria's One For The Money ("Penny"), a Sumer granddaughter. Tuesday would go on to be a multiple group winner and number-one Kuvasz for 2005. Penny became the top Kuvasz of the year for 2003 and 2004 and the national specialty winner in 2006. Penny is the first Kuvasz with a performance title to win a KCA BISS. Ch. Szumeria's Sealed With A Kiss RN won the first Generations Class to be held at a KCA specialty (2006) with her daughter Penny and Penny's seven-month-old daughter, Szumeria's Wildwood Penny From Heaven ("Angel") behind her. Angel was sired by outstanding conformation and

"Penny," formally Ch. Szumeria's One for the Money, stands proudly after being awarded the Group One title at the Des Moines Kennel Club in 2004.

performance winner Legend and won Winners Bitch, Best of Winners and Best Bred By Exhibitor at the 2006 specialty show. Angel went on to earn her championship the next month with a Best of Breed win, creating the very rare occurrence of having a mother and daughter ranked in the top twenty Kuvaszok of the year (for the first quarter of 2006).

Am./Can. Ch. Rocky Mountain Lady Bird (Bird) won the 2004 national. Awards of Merit went to Ch. Szumeria's That's My Story (a Ditto daughter) and Ch. Szumeria's Wildwood Ruby

Tuesday (a Nala granddaughter). Best of Opposite Sex went to Am./Can. Ch. Mauna Kea's Limited Release ("Shiraz"), a Markie son. Winners Bitch, Best of Winners and Best Puppy went to six-month-old Szumeria's Jager Kinsce ("Jade"). She was out of an import, Am./Hung. Ch. Vertesi Selymes Pengo (Pengo) and Rocky Mtn High Gambler At Szumeria ("Ben").

Breed history was made in 2005 when Ch. Szumeria's Legend CDX, RE, OA, NAP, OAJ, OJP became the first (and to date only) Kuvasz to qualify for five KCA

Performance Awards (Hall of Fame) in versatility, obedience, standard agility, jumpers agility and conformation, so he also carries behind his name these club awards: VOAA, OPA, SAPA, JAPA, CPA. Additionally, Legend maintains the distinct honor of being the only champion, as well as multiple Group-placing Kuvasz, to date, with advanced level AKC titles in both obedience and agility. He was awarded Best Veteran at the 2005 national and went on to win Best of Breed on the following day with his young daughter, Galaxy's Venus of Wildwood, as Best of Winners.

Two-thousand and five heralded the beginning of another great sport for Kuvasz when the AKC made rally obedience a titling event. Not to be outdone by other breeds, Kuvasz owners dove in and by the end of January, four new Rally Novice titles had been earned by Ch. Elso Szulott Kutya Hepnar RN, who later added a CD and RA; Ch. Elso Peachtree Alom RN; Sweet Harvest Bristol Breeze RN; and Szumeria's Starlight Express CD, RN, who later earned the first Rally Excellent title. By year's end, there were 25 new Rally Novice titles and 3 Rally Advanced. Kuvaszok were busy in other AKC performance disciplines as well. Ch. Mauna-Ederra's Double Image NA, OAJ had retired from the show ring but had come out in performance and followed up novice titles in agility with an Open Agility Jumpers title. The first Tracking Dog Excellent title for a Kuvasz was awarded to Ch. Brantwoods Harmony of Light TDX, who picked

A sixth Best in Show for Ch. Szumeria's Nala of Silverpick at the Vancouver Kennel Club in 2000 under judge Nancy Liebes.

up his CD and RN titles later in the year. The great performance Kuvasz, Kenai, retired from agility at the end of 2005 but not before earning a record number of titles and standing alone as the only Kuvasz to date to title at the Masters level. He is also the only Kuvasz to have been awarded a level 2 AKC Versatility Companion Dog, for titling in obedience, tracking, standard agility and jumpers agility. He is still out in the rally ring and the AKC titles after his name attest to his greatness: Rocky Mountain Summer Jazz VCD2, RA, MX, MXP3, MXJ, MJP5. He is the only recipient of the KCA's SAOAA and JAOAA for his agility achievements and has also been awarded the KCA, VOAA and OPA for versatility and obedience. Though no longer with us, a most notable Kuvasz in versatility was the multiple-Group-placing Ch. Mission's Brut Pezsgo Kiadas VCD1, OA, OAP, OAJ, AJP (Bubbles), owned by Lynn Vogel. Another Kuvasz renowned in versatility is retired veteran, Group-placing Ch. Starhavens Kaos of Solari CDX, NA, owned by LeAnn and Steven Miller.

Sumer, Nala and Pengo left their mark on the 2005 national through their descendants. The Best of Breed Winner was Ch. Szumeria's Native Son (Pengo bred to a Nala son), Best of Opposite Sex was Penny (a Sumer granddaughter) and Winners Bitch was Szumeria's Green Zaranath (a Sumer granddaughter).

Today, Ch. Szumeria's Jager Kinsce CPA ("Jade"), Ch. Glacier Creeks Whispering Wind CPA ("Brenda"), Ch. Double Ring New Southern Glory CPA (Glory) and Ch. Szumeria's Wildwood Ruby Tuesday COAA (Tuesday) are some of the top dogs making a run for the winner's circle in the breed ring. Ch. Szumeria's One For The Money COAA (Penny), is also in the race but is preparing for Agility and Obedience titles as well. Ch. Rocky Mountain Lady Bird (Bird) and Jade's brother, Ch Szumeria's The Buck Stops At Santa's Forest (Bucky), have puppies recently out of the whelping box. Through the miracle of modern science, two new Ditto puppies are practicing for the ring, as are other prospective stars of tomorrow. While all the contributors to the history of the breed in the US cannot be singled out for mention in this abbreviated account, the dogs and people that have been highlighted demonstrate how selective breeding has, in a few generations, resulted in the outstanding Kuvasz of today. Fanciers will be keeping an eye out for that next big show, breeding or performance winner, as the future of the breed continues to flourish in the hands of reputable breeders, owners and KCA members.

CHARACTERISTICS OF THE

KUVASZ

There's nothing more irresistible than a Kuvasz puppy—that white ball of fluff with sparkling eyes and an indomitable spirit. And as the pup grows into his thick white fur and graceful gait, the Kuvasz becomes an intelligent family dog, keen guard dog and loyal companion dog. His strength and agility are matched only by his devotion to his family. This is a relatively low-maintenance breed, aside from the copious shedding. A Kuvasz can be serious, stable, goofy and mellow—personality traits run the gamut from individual to individual. This breed is typically affectionate and cuddly with its family but is aloof with strangers and doesn't take well to kennel life. A Kuvasz has to be well-socialized to accept people outside of his immediate family.

PHYSICAL TRAITS

The Kuvasz is a member of the AKC's Working Group. He has a fluid gait and an unexaggerated build that disguises the dog's incredible strength. This large, double-coated guard dog was bred to watch flocks of livestock and to brave any kind of weather and terrain. The male stands typically between 28 and 30 inches tall at the shoulder. The minimum height for a male is 26 inches; anything less is a disqualification in the show ring. Average females are slightly smaller at 26 to 28 inches tall at the shoulder; the female's

Kuvaszok are intelligent dogs and will learn quickly when you employ positive training methods.

minimum height in the show ring is 24 inches. Male Kuvaszok are normally between 100 and 115 pounds; female dogs weigh between 70 and 90 pounds. For either sex, the Kuvasz should be a little longer than tall.

This breed has a double coat that consists of a short, fine undercoat and a longer, coarser outer coat. The coarseness of the hair helps the coat to repel water and dirt, making it easy to keep clean. The coat is also basically odorless. Regular bathing isn't necessary; however, regular brushing is essential for a healthy coat and skin.

All Kuvaszok are white. While the coat does vary in many shades of white, pure white is best for the show ring. The skin of this breed is either dark gray or black, but a preference is shown to darker skin. The hair around the face of the dog is shorter, but a long mane grows from the neck and down along the male dog's chest (this does not occur in females). The body of the Kuvasz is covered in a shaggy, but not too long, coat. The tail and back of the thighs are covered in hair 4 to 6 inches in length. The entire body coat can vary from straight to very wavy but should never be curly.

This breed sheds a lot and isn't for someone who isn't willing to do a lot of vacuuming. You will have hair everywhere—that's a guarantee! Fortunately, this breed

The Kuvasz coat comes only in white and can be straight or wavy.

isn't known to slobber (unless you're holding a large steak in front of it, of course).

The Kuvasz's ears and tail are not docked. The tail hangs low, curves slightly up at the end and is covered in a lot of shaggy fur. The ears are V-shaped, hang close to the dog's head, are thick and are covered in short fur. The eyes are wide-set and almond-shaped. They are set at a slight angle. The eyes are usually brown; the darker the shade of brown, the better.

The breed's gait has a smooth, fluid elegance. When the Kuvasz moves, his feet remain very close to the ground. Interestingly, when the dog moves quickly, his front legs fall in front of one another beneath the dog's center, forming a single line of tracks rather than two sets. When the dog is moving, he should carry his head almost level with his back. When standing, he can hold his head any way he desires.

One interesting distinguishing

characteristic of the Kuvasz is that his toes stay firmly together, so they look more like cat paws. Despite the delicate appearance of the feet, the pads are thick and durable. For the show ring, the nails should be black (preferred, but not necessary). It is also acceptable for hair to grow between the toes, but less hair is better.

In terms of the show ring, there are some differences between the Hungarian standard, the American Kennel Club (AKC) standard and the Canadian Kennel Club (CKC) standard. Most of these differences are slight, a matter of the dog's being a half-inch smaller or a difference in how much a dog can deviate from the ideals of the guidelines and still be acceptable for showing. This doesn't make a difference to most companion-dog owners, but it might be important for someone planning to show his Kuvasz. The aforementioned description is based on the AKC standard.

A STOIC BREED

Because the Kuvasz is a working dog that was bred to spend long hours trotting after his livestock charges, he is reluctant to show signs of discomfort or pain. For this reason, Kuvasz owners should know their dogs' habits very well and be able to detect changes in behavior and movement.

TEMPERAMENT AND PERSONALITY

The Kuvasz is often described as watchful, dedicated, protective, independent, strong-willed, cautious, powerful and resilient, although personality does differ from dog to dog. Some might be more affectionate or aggressive than others, but all Kuvaszok have the innate desire to protect the people and the other animals that they consider "their own." This dog is particularly vigilant at night, when the outside environment is quieter, making common noises more distinct. These noises may be countered by loud barking, which will wake the whole house, perhaps even the whole block! Some owners run a fan or white-noise machine to drown out these normal noises at night.

On a farm or in the field, the Kuvasz will fight to the death to protect livestock from predators. In a home setting, this breed will gladly protect its home from intruders or any other threat, real or perceived. Kuvaszok are even known to protect neighboring houses and yards from strangers if there is no other dog watching that territory. This breed is constantly watching for signs of danger. This trait can pose a problem at times because everyone from the mailman to the babysitter may be seen as a threat. The Kuvasz is naturally suspicious of strangers. With training and socialization, these dogs can learn to be friendlier with people they don't know, though their natural protective ability will always shine through. All Kuvasz puppies should be socialized as early as possible, because the Kuvasz is not a breed that takes to everyone it meets.

The Kuvasz is generally decent with children in his own family. He seems to recognize the vulnerability of children and will watch over them. However, this desire to protect children can sometimes go awry. Children might behave or play in ways that confuse the Kuvasz, like yelling or screaming. The dog might mistake loud noises from children as distress cries and become very upset, or he may confuse play screaming with aggression. Either way, this could result in a lot of barking and agitation on the dog's part. Always supervise this breed's interaction with children, just to make sure that nothing goes wrong, especially with younger children. The Kuvasz is not a dog that takes well to having his hair or ears pulled, but neither do most dogs. Children should learn the appropriate ways to interact with any dog.

An owner should socialize the Kuvasz to other dogs during the important puppy-socialization period when the pup is most likely to accept new things. Most Kuvaszok will try to establish a pack order with another dog right away, often as the dominant dog;

this is typical canine behavior. Because the Kuvasz is a natural-born leader, he is likely to challenge other dogs in the household. Breed history shows that Kuvaszok had to work in tandem with other dogs to defend flocks of animals, so they are bred to be in the company of other dogs, but their strong-willed nature definitely makes early and abundant socialization a requirement. Some Kuvaszok do very well with other dogs away from home but won't tolerate new dogs in their territory. If a rescued Kuvasz is dog-aggressive, the owner should consult a trainer and begin positive-reinforcement training to help the dog become properly socialized. As for cats and the

The Kuvasz is by nature a breed protective of his owners. Proper socialization will result in a dog happy to meet new friends.

breed, house cats that a Kuvasz grows up with are fine, but strange cats that wander into the yard better think twice before they cross a Kuvasz.

Despite the fact that the Kuvasz is very independent, he does not make a good kennel or outside dog unless he is being used to guard livestock; in that case, the dog is content to do his job. In a family situation, the Kuvasz really does need to be around his humans. If left alone outside in the yard (securely fenced, of course) for extended periods, the dog is likely to bark loudly and continuously until someone comes out to entertain him or bring him inside. Kuvaszok get bored and lonely when they are not with their families, and they may become aggressive if frequently left alone. The Kuvasz should be an indoor dog, where he can closely monitor, interact with and protect his family. Also, when left in the yard alone, a Kuvasz is likely to try to find a way out, so a sturdy 6-foot-high fence (or higher) is essential.

TRAINABILITY

Before formal training begins, puppy socialization is essential for this breed. The pup should meet all kinds of people and animals and be introduced to all kinds of situations. This will make the dog far less fearful as an adult, which can temper aggression. A Kuvasz that lives an isolated life with little exposure to the outside world is likely to antagonize and drive off visitors. The Kuvasz pup should be taught to approach new situations, objects, people and animals with confidence.

When it comes to obedience, the Kuvasz will generally only take commands from the people he respects and considers his family and generally responds best to the "leader" of the pack, the adult human who trains him most often. He doesn't take well to being reprimanded by anyone other than his owner or immediate family. Everyone in the family should have a part in training the dog. If not, the dog may not respond to some family members, creating a problem in the household. Smaller people and children might have a difficult time on the other end of the leash with a rambunctious adolescent of this breed. It's important to begin leash and basic obedience training early.

The Kuvasz responds extremely well to praise. Positive reinforcement methods and rewards are the best way to teach this breed. However, instead of performing behaviors blindly, the Kuvasz is discerning and wants to understand the reason behind a behavior, unlike other breeds that will do nearly anything for a treat—though few Kuvaszok will turn down a tasty morsel! Repetition in training will often bore this breed, so a trainer should "mix it up."

Although the Kuvasz is a "rough-and-tumble" type of dog, he is sensitive and doesn't do well with heavy-handed training styles. Many individual dogs will regard harsh treatment with resentment, belligerence and fear (as would many other breeds). The Kuvasz always remains independent and maintains a sense of dignity. He does not do well with mistreatment or wrongful scolding from anyone, though he is a forgiving breed and will allow his owner a few mistakes. Much of the time, when the dog is being "stubborn," the owner finds that his training signals were incorrect and that the dog was actually doing what the owner had asked.

As with other dogs, remain consistent when training a Kuvasz or else the dog will become confused and frustrated. The dog either will not learn as quickly or worse, will learn the wrong behaviors. Further, because these dogs are intelligent and learn quickly, it's important to be consistent as the pup grows (or even with a rescued adult dog). An owner shouldn't allow something one day, such as a nap on the couch, only to change the rules the next day.

The Kuvasz is indeed a quick learner when trained by positive reinforcement, but lessons should be kept brief and varied so that the dog doesn't get bored. This isn't a breed that will follow orders just to get a reward. The Kuvasz needs a patient owner that he respects. He

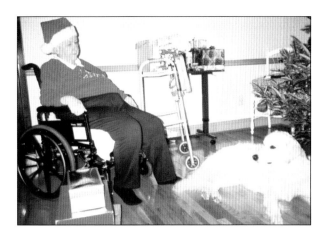

A properly trained Kuvasz can even excel at the role of therapy dog.

was bred to work independently in the field, so he can be stubborn with obedience, especially if a trainer uses a harsh training method.

House-training the Kuvasz is easy. While the puppy is still growing, he may have "accidents" in the house from time to time as his body changes, so it is essential to remain positive and reward successes. Most Kuvasz house-train fairly quickly if you remain consistent and give your pup frequent opportunities to "go" in the right place.

THE SPORTING KUVASZ
Kuvaszok compete in many sporting events, like conformation, agility, tracking and obedience. Conformation is the most traditional dog event; this is what most people refer to as the traditional "dog show." Dog shows are called conformation shows because they measure dogs based on how well they conform to their specific breed

standard. This includes their physical appearance, the way they move and their temperament. Dogs need to be trained in how to behave during the show, but, as the nature of this type of competition suggests, most of the qualities that the judges are looking for here are also inborn.

Conformation events do relate back to the Kuvasz as a guard dog. The physical build of the Kuvasz is what enables the breed to guard well. The dog's musculature and movements allow him to spring into action with the strength to fend off even the most threatening attacker. Keeping the breed within the guidelines of the standard ensures that quality Kuvasz, with the traits prized throughout the breed's history, will continue to be produced.

Agility is a type of performance competition that requires quite a bit of training, but the Kuvasz is up to the task. As the title of agility suggests, this competition tests to see how quickly and gracefully the dogs move, in this case over a series of obstacles. The correlation between this type of competition and the guarding world are a little more obvious: the Kuvasz must be fast, agile and quick-thinking while protecting animals in the field or people in the home. In any case, the Kuvasz's endurance makes him a good candidate for agility, though it takes a special trainer to gain the respect of this dog.

Obedience competition tests a dog's ability to perform a set of exercises at the direction of his handler. Though the Kuvasz is a worthy competitor in any sport, the breed is not an obedience superstar. Some individuals are incredibly motivated and easy to train while others don't perform well, preferring to wander off to check the perimeter of the yard or training area instead.

Kuvaszok also compete in tracking events, which are open to all breeds and test the dogs' natural scenting ability. The Kuvasz's history includes tracking game for hunters. As guard dogs, their sense of smell must be honed to everything in the environment, making tracking a natural sport for them.

The Kuvasz's powerful build make him a natural for drafting work. Having a friend cheering him on doesn't hurt either.

Kuvaszok can also become great therapy dogs, visiting patients in hospitals and nursing homes, though intense early socialization is essential if therapy work is something you'd like to consider. Since therapy dogs have to meet a lot of new and different kinds of people and are exposed to many different sights, sounds and situations, you'll want to introduce your Kuvasz puppy to all types of individuals and other dogs and take him to a variety of places. Official therapy dogs must first go through a testing process that determines their abilities and temperament.

HEALTH CONCERNS

Fortunately for the Kuvasz and his owner, this breed is naturally very healthy and not prone to many genetic problems. The breed's average lifespan is about 10 to 12 years, and some can live to be 14 or even older.

Owners should be very aware of their dog's movements and habits in order to detect health issues, as most of the problems affecting the breed are orthopedic. Because the Kuvasz will throw himself in harm's way to protect his family and property, the breed has developed an incredible tolerance for pain. The dog might limp slightly if injured, but may not make a big of a deal out of an injury, as other breeds might. The owner needs to be observant enough to discover a problem

ADDITIONAL HEALTH TIPS

The Kuvasz, being a large, deep-chested breed, is at risk of developing bloat, a potentially deadly condition in which the stomach twists on itself. Daily preventive measures must be incorporated into your Kuvasz's routine to protect him from bloat. The chapter on proper care discusses bloat in more detail in the sections on feeding. Allergic reactions to certain types of vaccines and to penicillin also have been reported in the Kuvasz, as well as sensitivity to anesthesia. Discuss these drug reactions with your breeder so that you can inform your vet. Your vet must be made aware of these issues from the outset so that he can treat your Kuvasz safely. Discuss which types of medications your Kuvasz is getting, and be aware that penicillin is used as a preservative in some vaccines. Thyroid problems are a current focus of research in the breed as well. The Kuvasz Club of America has a health committee that is dedicated to Kuvasz health issues and finding out as much as possible about the problems in the breed, causes behind them, treatment and prevention.

should one occur. This breed is prone to cruciate ligament injury especially in the back legs, the primary symptom of which is lameness and favoring of the painful limb.

Like most large breeds, the

Do You Know about Hip Dysplasia?

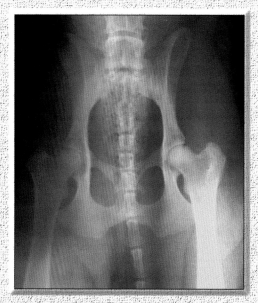

X-ray of a dog with "Good" hips.

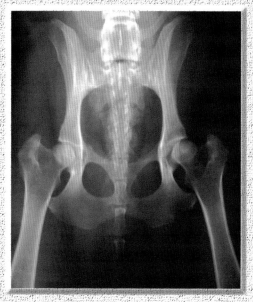

X-ray of a dog with "Moderate" dysplastic hips.

Hip dysplasia is a fairly common condition found in pure-bred dogs. When a dog has hip dysplasia, his hind leg has an incorrectly formed hip joint. By constant use of the hip joint, it becomes more and more loose, wears abnormally and may become arthritic.

Hip dysplasia can only be confirmed with an x-ray, but certain symptoms may indicate a problem. Your dog may have a hip dysplasia problem if he walks in a peculiar manner, hops instead of smoothly runs, uses his hind legs in unison (to keep the pressure off the weak joint), has trouble getting up from a prone position or always sits with both legs together on one side of his body.

As the dog matures, he may adapt well to life with a bad hip, but in a few years the arthritis develops and many dogs with hip dysplasia become crippled.

Hip dysplasia is considered an inherited disease and can be diagnosed definitively by x-ray only when the dog is two years old, although symptoms often appear earlier. Some experts claim that a special diet might help your puppy outgrow the bad hip, but the usual treatments are surgical. The removal of the pectineus muscle, the removal of the round part of the femur, reconstructing the pelvis and replacing the hip with an artificial one are all surgical interventions that are expensive, but they are usually very successful. Follow the advice of your veterinarian.

Kuvasz can encounter hip dysplasia, an arthritic disorder with genetic roots. Improperly developed cartilage causes arthritic symptoms which can happen in other joints, but the hips are the most commonly stricken areas. Because diet and exercise also contribute to the onset of hip dysplasia, it's essential to offer the best food in the proper amounts and not to allow a young Kuvasz to have strenuous or prolonged exercise. If dogs are kept at a healthy weight and exercised appropriately, symptoms can be manageable in a dog that already shows the beginnings of the disease. There are also medications available to help the dog manage pain and try to reduce inflammation around the joint. Before you buy a puppy, make sure that the breeder had both the sire and dam tested for hip dysplasia and that the results were acceptable based on the require- ments from the Orthopedic Foundation for Animals (OFA). Ask the breeder to show you documenta- tion of OFA hip clearances for both parents, as dysplastic dogs should never be bred. You can also search the OFA's records and learn more about testing at www.offa.org.

The Kuvasz Club of America (KCA) has joined the CHIC (Canine Health Information Center) program through the Canine Health Foundation, whose tests determine the health of the hips, elbows and thyroid. In order for a Kuvasz to earn a CHIC number, it has to be

HEART-HEALTHY
In this modern age of ever-improving cardio-care, no doctor or scientist can dispute the advantages of owning a dog to lower a person's risk of heart disease. Studies have proven that petting a dog, walking a dog and grooming a dog all show positive results toward lowering your blood pressure. The simple routine of exercising your dog—going outside with the dog and walking, jogging or playing catch—is heart-healthy in and of itself. If you are normally less active than your physician thinks you should be, adopting a dog may be a smart option to improve your own quality of life as well as that of another creature.

tested through this organization (the number is also listed in the OFA's database). Other tests are recommended, such as those for eye disease, knee problems, heart disease and von Willebrand's disease (a blood-clotting disorder). Prospective Kuvasz owners can search the CHIC database for health clearances on the parents of any puppy, as well as his relatives. Visit CHIC online at www.caninehealth- info.org.

Osteochondritis dissecans (OCD) is an orthopedic problem affecting the shoulder joints of the dog, but it can also afflict other joints. With OCD, a flap of cartilage forms on the joint, rubbing against other parts of the joint when it is flexed, causing pain and crippling

Despite having a more independent personality than many dogs, the Kuvasz still relies on your care—especially as a puppy.

These things can contribute to the onset of many orthopedic disorders.

Because this is a large breed that is slow to develop, take care not to exercise dogs under 18 months too vigorously, or bone problems can occur. For this reason, the Kuvasz doesn't make a great jogging partner. Try to have the pup avoid repeated stair climbing or hiking in rough terrain. The Kuvasz does need exercise, though, so regular walks and ball playing in the yard are great. Appropriate exercise for good joint health is essential and helps the puppy to "blow off steam."

THE IDEAL OWNER

The ideal owner for the Kuvasz is someone with the time and patience to properly train and socialize his dog. This could be said of any dog, but a large protective breed like this one requires an owner dedicated to training. An owner will have to work to earn the dog's respect and obedience, establishing a pack order from the beginning, with the human at the top. Fear and physically forceful training aren't good tactics for this breed and will definitely backfire. Instead, reward wanted behaviors and don't reward unwanted behaviors. Being "top dog" does not mean physical roughness. Instead, use behaviors that your dog will understand, such as feeding him after you eat, making the dog sit before he goes in and out of doors and not allowing him up on the furniture unless invited.

effects. Most dogs affected by OCD develop the disorder between four and nine months of age. Osteochondritis dissecans can be treated with medication and possibly surgery, and owners should seek veterinary attention at the first sign of lameness. The sooner treatment begins, the easier it is for the dog to heal.

Hypertrophic osteodystrophy (HOD) and panosteitis (familiarly called "growing pains") are two bone disorders that are only rarely seen in the Kuvasz. Both conditions cause lameness, and HOD can progress to cause permanent damage. It is important not to feed a Kuvasz a diet too high in protein or one that encourages rapid growth and not to oversupplement the diet.

The Kuvasz is great for people interested in a guard dog or family protector and companion. However, this is not a breed that does well when left alone. A Kuvasz may not be a "lap dog" (though he may try to be!), but he is definitely a family dog and likes to cuddle and be petted. Kuvaszok that are used to guard livestock do well without their human companions because they have the livestock and often other dogs for company, and they love to do their job.

The Kuvasz is not the ideal breed for people with many children or many other dogs. A Kuvasz may want to take over the household, and kids and other animals may not know how to deal with this strong temperament. The problem isn't the kids—the problem is the kids' behavior and lack of supervision. Children should be taught to behave calmly around any dog and to treat the animal with respect. Small children should be supervised around any dog. The Kuvasz will be fine with a family of well-behaved, supervised children, but remember that he is suspicious of all strangers, and that includes other children. A Kuvasz who is gentle with the children in his family may not act the same way toward children he does not know, making supervision of the utmost importance.

This breed needs adequate exercise, at least 30 minutes twice a day at minimum. The Kuvasz also doesn't do particularly well in small spaces, so he doesn't make a great city or apartment dog unless owners make sure to provide exercise and several walks each day. A fenced-in yard is important for exercise and to contain the dog. The Kuvasz tends to wander if he gets out of the house, so be certain to watch the dog when the doors are open. Even an electric invisible fence will not stop this breed from leaving the yard.

Ideally, the Kuvasz prefers a cool climate or a place that's cool for much of the year. This breed is uncomfortable in warm weather but does great in cold and snow as long as he has shelter. However, Kuvaszok that live in warm climates become savvy about finding the coolest spots in the house and are known to hang out around air-conditioner vents. Therefore, a Kuvasz in southern Florida can do just a well as one in Alaska, as long as the owner takes care to make the dog comfortable.

The Kuvasz's coat is designed to withstand the cold, and the breed will actually be more comfortable in the snow than in the heat.

KUVASZ

WHAT IS A BREED STANDARD?
A breed standard is an official document that provides a written description of the ideal characteristics of its breed: the physical traits, personality, movement and inherent abilities that make the breed what it is and distinguish it from other breeds. The American Kennel Club's (AKC) breed standards are written by members of each breed's parent club and submitted for approval. In the US, the parent club for the Kuvasz is the Kuvasz Club of America.

The breed standard provides indispensable guidelines to breeders as they strive to preserve their breed in its true form from generation to generation, as well as to conformation show judges as they choose the dog that best represents the ideal for the breed as the winner. We've mentioned how standards of different countries and kennel clubs around the world can vary on certain points, but in essence all standards should describe the same dogs.

A dog in profile of good coat and substance, well balanced, correct structure and type.

Of course, words are open to individual interpretation, so one must learn to recognize what the words in the standard mean by observing quality Kuvaszok in action.

THE AMERICAN KENNEL CLUB STANDARD FOR THE KUVASZ

General Appearance: A working dog of larger size, sturdily built, well balanced, neither lanky nor cobby. White in color with no markings. Medium boned, well muscled, without the slightest hint of bulkiness or lethargy. Impresses the eye with strength and activity combined with light-footedness, moves freely on strong legs. The following description is that of the ideal Kuvasz. Any deviation must be penalized to the extent of the deviation.

Size, Proportion, Substance: *Height* measured at the withers—dogs, 28 to 30 inches; bitches, 26 to 28 inches. *Disqualifications*—dogs smaller than 26 inches. Bitches smaller than 24 inches. *Weight*—dogs approximately 100 to 115 pounds, bitches approximately 70 to 90 pounds. Trunk and limbs form a horizontal rectangle slightly deviated from the square. Bone in proportion to size of body. Medium, hard. Never heavy or coarse. Any tendency to weakness or lack of substance is a decided fault.

Head: Proportions are of great importance as the head is considered to be the most beautiful part of the Kuvasz. Length of head measured from tip of nose to occiput is slightly less than half the height of the dog at the withers. Width is half the length of the head. *Eyes*—almond-shaped, set well apart, somewhat slanted. In profile, the eyes are set slightly below the plane of the muzzle. Lids tight, haws should not show. Dark brown, the darker the better. *Ears*—V-shaped, tip is slightly rounded. Rather thick, they are well set back between the

Head study with correct proportion, structure and type with a pleasing expression.

FAULTS IN PROFILE

Generally lacking bone and substance, too high on leg, flat feet, weak pasterns, lacking sufficient angulation front and rear, high in the rear.

Roman nose and lacking stop, short neck, weak front, toes out, soft topline, weak rear and cow hocked, flat feet.

Upright shoulders, dip behind withers and high in rear, weak rear lacking angulation, shallow chested, tail incorrectly carried over back.

Too much bone and substance, low on leg, lacking athletic outline typical of the Kuvasz, ring tail.

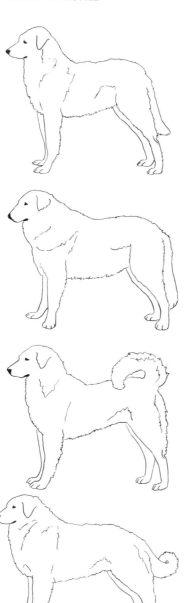

level of the eye and the top of the head. When pulled forward the tip of the ear should cover the eye. Looking at the dog face to face, the widest part of the ear is about level to the eye. The inner edge of the ear lies close to the cheek, the outer edge slightly away from the head forming a V. In the relaxed position, the ears should hold their set and not cast backward. The ears should not protrude above the head. The skull is elongated but not pointed. The stop is defined, never abrupt, raising the forehead gently above the plane of the muzzle. The longitudinal midline of the forehead is pronounced, widening as it slopes to the muzzle. *Cheeks*—flat, bony arches above the eyes. The skin is dry. *Muzzle*—length in proportion to the length of the head, top straight, not pointed, underjaw well developed. Inside of the mouth preferably black. *Nose*—large, black nostrils well opened. Lips black, closely covering the teeth. The upper lip covers tightly the upper jaw only; no excess flews. Lower lip tight and not pendulous. *Bite*—dentition full, scissors bite preferred. Level bite acceptable. *Disqualifications*—overshot bite, undershot bite.

Neck, Topline, Body: *Neck*—muscular, without dewlap, medium length, arched at the crest. *Back*—of medium length,

The breed standard describes the Kuvasz as devoted, gentle and patient, an accurate depiction of this talented and beautiful companion dog.

straight, firm and quite broad. The loin is short, muscular and tight. The *croup* well muscled, slightly sloping. *Forechest* is well developed. When viewed from the side, the forechest protrudes slightly in front of the shoulders. *Chest*—deep with long, well-sprung ribs reaching almost to the elbows. The *brisket* is deep, well developed and runs parallel to the ground. The *stomach* is well tucked up. *Tail*—carried low, natural length reaching at least to the hocks. In repose it hangs down resting on the body, the end but slightly lifted. In state of excitement, the tail may be elevated to the level of the loin, the tip slightly curved up. Ideally there should not be much difference in the carriage of the tail in state of excitement or in repose.

Forequarters: *Shoulders*—muscular and long. *Topline*—withers are higher than the back. The scapula and humerus form a right angle, are long and of equal length. Elbows neither in nor out. Legs are medium boned, straight and well muscled. The joints are dry, hard. Dewclaws on the forelegs should not be removed. Feet well padded. Pads resilient, black. Feet are closed tight, forming round "cat feet." Some hair between the toes, the less the better. Dark nails are preferred.

Hindquarters: The portion behind the hip joint is moderately long, producing wide, long and strong muscles of the upper thigh. The femur is long, creating well-bent stifles. Lower thigh is long, dry, well muscled. Metatarsus is short, broad and of great strength. Dewclaws, if any, are removed. Feet as in front, except the rear paws somewhat longer.

Coat: The Kuvasz has a double coat, formed by guard hair and fine undercoat. The texture of the coat is medium coarse. The coat ranges from quite wavy to straight. Distribution follows a definite pattern over the body regardless of coat type. The head, muzzle, ears and paws are covered with short, smooth hair. The neck has a mane that extends to and covers the chest. Coat on the front of the forelegs up to the elbows and the hind legs below the thighs is short and smooth. The backs of the forelegs are feathered to the pastern with hair 2 to 3 inches long. The body and sides of the thighs are covered with a medium length coat. The back of the thighs and the entire tail are covered with hair 4 to 6 inches long. It is natural for the Kuvasz to lose most of the long coat during hot weather. Full luxuriant coat comes in seasonally, depending on climate. Summer coat should not be penalized.

Color: White. The skin is heavily pigmented. The more slate gray or black pigmentation the better.

Gait: Easy, free and elastic. Feet travel close to the ground. Hind legs reach far under, meeting or even passing the imprints of the front legs. Moving toward an observer, the front legs do not travel parallel to each other, but rather close together at the ground. When viewed from the rear, the hind legs (from the hip joint down) also move close to the ground. As speed increases, the legs gradually angle more inward until the pads are almost single-tracking. Unless excited, the head is carried rather low at the level of the shoulders. Desired movement cannot be maintained without sufficient angulation and firm slimness of body.

Temperament: A spirited dog of keen intelligence, determination, courage and curiosity. Very sensitive to praise and blame. Primarily a one-family dog. Devoted, gentle and patient without being overly demonstrative. Always ready to protect loved ones even to the point of self-sacrifice. Extremely strong instinct to protect children. Polite to accepted strangers, but rather suspicious and very discriminating in making new friends. Unexcelled guard, possessing ability to act on his own initiative at just the right moment without instruction. Bold, courageous and fearless.

Untiring ability to work and cover rough terrain for long periods of time. Has good scent and has been used to hunt game.

Disqualifications: Overshot bite. Undershot bite. *Dogs*—smaller than 26 inches. *Bitches*—smaller than 24 inches.

Approved July 12, 1999
Effective August 30, 1999

The main reason that standards exist is to protect the desired type of the breed.

KUVASZ

FINDING YOUR KUVASZ

Finding a Kuvasz breeder is the best way to get a puppy. Good breeders are constantly trying to improve the breed and produce healthier dogs for the future. Of course, going to a breeder is no guarantee of getting a dog that's a perfect fit for your family, but it is a good start. If you can meet your pup's parents, you will have a

With one Kuvasz puppy being cuter than the next, you may wish to bring them all home. A quality breeder will help you choose the pup that will be the perfect fit for your household.

good idea of what your dog will be like when he becomes an adult.

Some breeders want to competitively show most of their "good" puppies and will only sell pups that they feel won't do well in the show ring. Perhaps the pup is too small or has the wrong eye color. These traits don't really matter in a family dog, so don't worry if your puppy doesn't fit the standard perfectly. These small cosmetic faults only affect the puppy's breedability, not his looks, health, pet quality or guarding behavior.

Rescue organizations are another great way to find a Kuvasz, as these groups take in Kuvaszok who for some reason find themselves in need of new homes. Dogs from rescue groups are generally adults. These dogs are a little more likely to have temperament or training issues. Rescue dogs are not bad dogs, but they may have been mistreated or undersocialized and therefore require a lot of loving compassion and dedication to their training. In most cases, lack of training is what lands the Kuvasz in a rescue, which is hardly the dog's fault. Sometimes it's simply a case of the owners moving, a new baby, allergies, etc. Luckily, with time and training, rescue dogs normally become loving family pets. A rescue organization will generally not place an aggressive dog, so you can be relatively certain that a "secondhand" Kuvasz will have a decent temperament. Rescues evaluate the dogs and the families who apply to adopt them carefully so that the individual dog can be matched with the correct family.

Whether you have your heart set on a puppy or you are looking to adopt an adult Kuvasz, you should begin your search with the Kuvasz Club of America. They operate a rescue program and also provide a breeders' list on their website so you can find a member breeder in your region of the country. Member breeders

included on this list have agreed to follow the club's code of conduct in their breeding programs.

True breed fanciers are out to improve the breed and will help you choose the right puppy for your household. You'll not only gain a puppy, you'll gain a mentor as well. In any case, the Kuvasz isn't a well-known breed, so the likelihood of finding a puppy from a source other than a breeder is slim. Regardless, a breeder or breed rescue should be the only places from which you consider obtaining a Kuvasz.

Going to a breeder and meeting the sire and dam of the puppy increase the odds of getting a healthy pup with a good temperament. The parents of the puppy are a good indicator of what the puppy will be like when he grows up. If the parents are friendly and healthy, the

TEMPERAMENT ABOVE ALL ELSE

Regardless of breed, a puppy's disposition is perhaps his most important quality. It is, after all, what makes a puppy lovable and "livable." If the puppy's parents or grandparents are known to be snappy or aggressive, the puppy is likely to inherit those tendencies. That can lead to serious problems, such as the dog's becoming a biter, which can lead to eventual abandonment.

Remember that the puppy you select will grow up to be a part of your family for years to come, so take your time in making the selection. Do some research and use your head, not just your heart.

puppy most likely will be too, especially if the breeder is conscientious and has begun to socialize the pups early.

Also consider genetic issues when getting a puppy. Although the Kuvasz is a relatively healthy breed, it can still have joint problems, like hip dysplasia, and other orthopedic issues related to its size and growth. All registered dogs, like those of a reputable breeder, should be certified by the Orthopedic Foundation for Animals (OFA). The OFA checks dogs for hip dysplasia and rates them accordingly from "poor" to "excellent." Only buy a dog whose parents were both rated "fair," "good" or "excellent." This is no guarantee that a puppy will not have joint problems, but it certainly is a good indication of genetic health. The OFA maintains databases for other genetic disorders, and many good breeders test for these as well. Ask to see all health-testing documentation on the parents of the litter you are observing.

Before getting a Kuvasz puppy, consider whether you want a male or female. Males average about 15 to 20 pounds heavier than females. Once you've made that decision, meet the litter of pups and pick each one up, looking for those that feel solid and sturdy; hopefully all of them will. The pups should be active and alert (when it's not nap time, of course). Watch to see how the pups react to various noises, toys and stimuli. Choose a puppy that isn't fearful of new things.

Along with the process of your choosing a good breeder and puppy, comes the breeder's process of selecting you as a good owner and caretaker of one of his puppies. The breeder will have

MALE OR FEMALE?

Males of most dog breeds tend to be larger than their female counterparts and take longer to mature. Males also can be more dominant and territorial, especially if they are intact. Neutering before one year of age can help minimize those tendencies. Females of most breeds are often less rambunctious and easier to handle. However, individual personalities vary, so the differences are often due more to temperament than to the sex of the animal.

many questions for you, so be sure to do your homework on the breed and be prepared for the commitment of dog ownership. Hopefully the breeder will deem you a worthy owner of one of his pups and agree to sell you a puppy. When you purchase the puppy, you will also get his registration papers, a copy of his pedigree, a certificate of vaccinations and any other health records and a copy of the breeder's sales agreement, which may guarantee against any health defects for a certain period of time. Many good breeders also include literature about feeding and other aspects of raising a Kuvasz puppy.

Puppies will be dependent on their owner for the care that will keep them healthy and sound throughout their lives, so be certain that you have the time and devotion to give.

A SHOW PUPPY

If you plan to show your puppy, you must first deal with a reputable breeder who shows his dogs and has had some success in the conformation ring. The puppy's pedigree should include one or more champions in the first and second generation. You should be familiar with the breed and breed standard so you can know what qualities to look for in your puppy. The breeder's observations and recommendations also are invaluable aids in selecting your future champion. If you consider an older puppy, be sure that the puppy has been properly socialized with people and not isolated in a kennel without substantial daily human contact.

A COMMITTED NEW OWNER

By now you should understand what makes the Kuvasz a most unique and special dog, one that may fit nicely into your family and lifestyle. If you have researched breeders, you should be able to recognize a knowledgeable and responsible Kuvasz breeder who cares not only about his pups but also about what kind of owner you will be. If you have completed the final step in your new journey, you have found a litter, or possibly two, of quality Kuvasz pups.

A visit with the puppies and their breeder should be an education in itself. Breed research, breeder selection and puppy visitation are very

COST OF OWNERSHIP
The purchase price of your puppy is merely the first expense in the typical dog budget. Quality dog food, veterinary care (sickness and health maintenance), dog supplies and grooming costs will add up to big bucks every year. Can you adequately afford to support a canine addition to the family?

important aspects of finding the puppy of your dreams. Beyond that, these things also lay the foundation for a successful future with your pup. Puppy personalities within each litter vary, from the shy and easygoing puppy to the one who is dominant and assertive, with most pups falling somewhere in between. By spending time with the puppies

you will be able to recognize certain behaviors and what these behaviors indicate about each pup's temperament. Which type of pup will complement your family dynamics is best determined by observing the puppies in action within their "pack." Your breeder's expertise and recommendations are also valuable. Although you may fall in love with a bold and brassy male, the breeder may suggest that another pup would be best for you. The breeder's experience in rearing Kuvasz pups and matching their temperaments with appropriate humans offers the best assurance that your pup will meet your needs and expectations. The type of puppy that you select is just as important as your decision that the Kuvasz is the breed for you.

Kuvasz puppies are quite the investigators. They will stick their noses—literally—into whatever captures their interest.

The decision to live with a Kuvasz is a serious commitment and not one to be taken lightly. This puppy is a living sentient being that will be dependent on you for basic survival for his entire life. Beyond the basics of survival—food, water, shelter and protection—he needs much, much more. The new pup needs love, nurturing and a proper canine education to mold him into a responsible, well-behaved canine citizen. Your Kuvasz's health and good manners will need consistent monitoring and regular "tune-ups," so your job as a responsible dog owner will be ongoing throughout every stage of his life. If you are not prepared to accept these responsibilities and commit to them for the next decade, likely longer, then you are not prepared to own a dog of any breed.

Although the responsibilities of owning a dog may at times tax your patience, the joy of living with your Kuvasz far outweighs the workload, and a well-mannered adult dog is worth your time and effort. Before your very eyes, your new charge will grow up to be your most loyal friend, devoted to you unconditionally.

YOUR KUVASZ SHOPPING LIST

Just as expectant parents prepare a nursery for their baby, so should you ready your home for the arrival of your Kuvasz pup. If you have the necessary puppy

It's dinner for two for these Kuvasz puppies.

supplies purchased and in place before he comes home, it will ease the puppy's transition from the warmth and familiarity of his mom and littermates to the brand-new environment of his new home and human family. You will be too busy to stock up and prepare your house after your pup comes home, that's for sure! Imagine how a pup must feel upon being transported to a strange new place. It's up to you to comfort him and to let your little pup know that he is going to be happy with you.

FOOD AND WATER BOWLS

Your puppy will need separate bowls for his food and water. Stainless steel pans are generally preferred over plastic bowls since they sterilize better and

Stainless steel bowls are a wise choice, as they are less attractive for pups to chew on.

pups are less inclined to chew on the metal. Heavy-duty ceramic bowls are popular, but consider how often you will have to pick up those heavy bowls. Buy adult-sized pans, as your puppy will grow into them before you know it.

THE DOG CRATE

If you think that crates are tools of punishment and confinement for when a dog has misbehaved, think again. Most breeders and almost all trainers recommend a crate as the preferred house-training aid as well as for all-around puppy training and safety. Because dogs are natural den creatures that prefer cave-like environments, the benefits of crate use are many. The crate provides the puppy with his very own "safe house," a cozy place to sleep, take a break or seek comfort with a favorite toy; a travel aid to house your dog when on the road, at motels or at the vet's office; a training aid to help teach your puppy proper toileting habits; and a place of solitude when non-dog people happen to drop by and don't want a lively puppy—or even a well-behaved adult dog—saying hello or begging for attention.

When pups are small they will be able to spend time with their dams in the crate, which will better prepare them for the "den" you will provide them with after they leave the kennel.

Crates come in several types, although the wire crate and the fiberglass airline-type crate are the most popular. Both are safe and your puppy will adjust to either one, so the choice is up to you. The wire crates offer better visibility for the pup as well as better ventilation. Many of the wire crates easily collapse into suitcase-size carriers. The fiberglass crates, similar to those used by the airlines for animal transport, are sturdier and more den-like. However, the fiberglass crates do not collapse and are less ventilated than a wire crate, which can be problematic in hot weather. Some of the newer crates are made of heavy plastic mesh; they are very lightweight and fold up into slim-line suitcases.

CRATE EXPECTATIONS

To make the crate more inviting to your puppy, you can offer his first meal or two inside the crate, always keeping the crate door open so that he does not feel confined. Keep a favorite toy or two in the crate for him to play with while inside. You can also cover the crate at night with a lightweight sheet to make it more den-like and remove the stimuli of household activity. Never put him into his crate as punishment or as you are scolding him, since he will then associate his crate with negative situations and avoid going there.

However, a mesh crate might not be suitable for a pup with manic chewing habits.

Don't bother with a puppy-sized crate. Although your Kuvasz will be a little fellow when you bring him home, he will grow up in the blink of an eye and your puppy crate will be useless. Keeping in mind that a Kuvasz can be around 30 inches tall at the shoulder, depending on sex and the individual dog. You will need an extra-large crate that will allow him to fully stand, lie down and turn around at his full adult size. To help with house-training and create a den-like space for the Kuvasz puppy, removable divider panels can be used to partition the crate into a smaller area for the youngster.

You need to provide your Kuvasz puppy with a comfortable and safe place to sleep—and plenty of safe toys to boot.

BEDDING AND CRATE PADS

Your puppy will enjoy some type of soft bedding in his "room" (the

TOYS 'R SAFE

The vast array of tantalizing puppy toys is staggering. Stroll through any pet shop or pet-supply outlet and you will see that the choices can be overwhelming. However, not all dog toys are safe or sensible. Most very young puppies enjoy soft woolly toys that they can snuggle with and carry around. (You know they have outgrown them when they shred them up!) Avoid toys that have buttons, tabs or other enhancements that can be chewed off and swallowed. Soft toys that squeak are fun, but make sure your puppy does not disembowel the toy and remove (and swallow) the squeaker. Toys that rattle or make noise can excite a puppy, but they present the same danger as the squeaky kind and so require supervision. Hard rubber toys that bounce can also entertain a pup, but make sure that the toy is too big for your pup to swallow.

crate), something he can snuggle into to feel cozy and secure. Old towels or blankets are good choices for a young pup, since he may (and probably will) have a toileting accident or two in the crate or decide to chew on the bedding material. Once he is fully trained and out of the early chewing stage, you can replace the puppy bedding with a permanent crate pad if you prefer. Crate pads and other dog beds run the gamut from inexpensive to high-end doggie-designer styles, but don't splurge on the good stuff until you are sure that your puppy is reliable and won't tear it up or make a mess on it.

PUPPY TOYS

Just as infants and older children require objects to stimulate their minds and bodies, puppies need toys to entertain their curious brains, wiggly paws and achy teeth. A fun array of safe doggie toys will help satisfy your puppy's chewing instincts and distract him from gnawing on the leg of your antique chair or your new leather sofa. Most puppy toys are cute and look as if they would be a lot of fun, but not all are necessarily safe or good for your puppy, so use caution when you go puppy-toy shopping.

Kuvasz are strong dogs with strong teeth and jaws. The best "chewcifiers" are nylon and hard rubber bones, which are safe to gnaw on and come in sizes appropriate for all age groups and breeds. Be especially careful of natural bones, which can splinter or develop dangerous sharp edges; pups can easily swallow or choke on those bone splinters. Veterinarians often tell of surgical nightmares involving bits of splintered bone, because in addition to the danger of choking, the sharp pieces can damage the intestinal tract if swallowed.

Similarly, rawhide chews, while a favorite of most dogs and puppies, can be equally dangerous. Pieces of rawhide are easily swallowed after they get soft and gummy from chewing, and dogs have been known to choke on pieces of ingested rawhide. Rawhide chews should be offered only when you can supervise the puppy.

Soft woolly toys are special puppy favorites. They come in a wide variety of cute shapes and sizes; some look like little stuffed animals. Puppies love to shake them up and toss them about or simply carry them around. Be careful of fuzzy toys that have

Providing your pup with chew toys is especially beneficial when outdoors. Just think of all the dangerous things he can get his mouth on out there.

Dogs of all ages enjoy a good chew, so provide your pup with plenty of safe chew toys.

button eyes or noses that your pup could chew off and swallow, and make sure that he does not disembowel a squeaky toy to remove the squeaker! Braided rope toys are similar in that they are fun to chew and toss around,

but they shred easily and the strings are easy to swallow. The strings are not digestible and, if the puppy doesn't pass them in his stool, he could end up at the vet's office. As with rawhides, your puppy should be closely monitored with rope toys.

If you believe that your pup has ingested a piece of one of his toys, check his stool for the next couple of days to see if he passes the item when he defecates. At the same time, also watch for signs of intestinal distress. A call to your veterinarian might be in order to get his advice and be on the safe side.

An all-time favorite toy for puppies (young and old!) is the empty gallon milk jug. Hard plastic juice containers—46 ounces or more—are also excellent. Such containers make lots of noise when they are batted about, and puppies go crazy with delight as they play with them. However, they don't last very long, so be sure to remove and replace them when they get chewed up.

A word of caution about homemade toys: be careful with your choices of non-traditional play objects. Never use old shoes or socks, since a puppy cannot distinguish between the old ones on which he's allowed to chew and the new ones in your closet that are strictly off limits. That principle applies to anything that resembles something that you don't want your puppy to chew.

COLLARS

A lightweight nylon collar is the best choice for a very young pup. Quick-click collars are easy to put on and remove, and they can be adjusted as the puppy grows. Introduce him to his collar as soon as he comes home to get him accustomed to wearing it. He'll

TAKE THE LEAD

When teaching a pup to walk on lead, don't fight him as he flips about and tries to get away. Just stand and talk to him calmly, and dangle a treat in front of him. Start walking. He will usually follow your hand with the treat. Keep the session very short, and use a buckle collar (no choke for the puppy!). There are also head leads, which fit on the head instead of the neck (where the head goes, the body must follow). Dogs usually fight this at first, as it seems like a muzzle, but they soon adjust and seem to feel comfortable.

get used to it quickly and won't mind a bit. Make sure that it is snug enough that it won't slip off, yet loose enough to be comfortable for the pup. You should be able to slip two fingers between the collar and his neck. Check the collar often, as puppies grow in spurts, and his collar can become too tight almost overnight.

Leashes

A 6-foot nylon lead is an excellent choice for a young puppy. It is lightweight and not as tempting to chew as a leather lead. You can switch to a 6-foot leather lead after your pup has grown and is used to walking politely on a lead. For initial puppy walks and house-training purposes, you should invest in a shorter lead so

that you have more control over the puppy. At first, you don't want him wandering too far away from you, and when taking him out for toileting you will want to keep him in the specific area chosen for his potty spot.

HOME SAFETY FOR PUPPY

The importance of puppy-proofing cannot be overstated. In addition to making your house comfortable for your Kuvasz's arrival, you also must make sure that your house is safe for your puppy before you bring him home. There are countless hazards in the owner's personal living environment that a pup can sniff, chew, swallow or destroy. Many are obvious; others are not. Do a thorough advance

Your Kuvasz puppy should be supervised whenever he's playing outdoors. Be sure that you have puppy-proofed your yard before the puppy arrives home.

house check to remove or rearrange those things that could hurt your puppy, keeping any potentially dangerous items out of areas to which he will have access.

Electrical cords are especially dangerous, since puppies view them as irresistible chew toys. Unplug and remove all exposed cords or fasten them beneath baseboards where the puppy cannot reach them. Veterinarians and firefighters can tell you horror stories about electrical burns and house fires that resulted from puppy-chewed electrical cords. Consider this a most serious precaution for your puppy and the rest of your family.

Scout your home for tiny objects that might be seen at a pup's eye level and realize that the Kuvasz grows tall very quickly, and more and more will be within his reach. Keep medication bottles and cleaning supplies well out of reach, and do the same with waste baskets and other trash containers. It goes without saying that you should not use rodent poison or other toxic chemicals in any puppy area and that you must keep such containers safely locked up. You will be amazed at how many places a curious puppy can discover!

Once your house has cleared inspection, check your yard. A sturdy fence, well embedded into the ground, will give your dog a safe place to play and potty. Kuvaszok are known to be escape artists, so a fence of at least 6 feet high will be necessary to contain an agile youngster or adult. Check the fence periodically for necessary repairs. If there is a weak link or space to squeeze through, you can be sure a determined Kuvasz will discover it. Likewise, be careful when entering and exiting the house that your dog does not get out through the open door. Teaching commands like "Stay" and "Wait" can be helpful for this as well.

The garage and shed can be hazardous places for a pup, as things like fertilizers, chemicals and tools are usually kept there. It's best to keep these areas off limits to the pup. Antifreeze is especially dangerous to dogs, as they find the taste appealing and it takes only a few licks from the driveway to kill a dog, puppy or adult, small breed or large.

VISITING THE VETERINARIAN
A good veterinarian is your Kuvasz puppy's best health-insurance policy. If you do not already have a vet, ask your breeder, friends and experienced dog people in your area for recommendations so that you can select a vet, preferably one experienced in large-breed dogs, before you bring your Kuvasz puppy home. Also arrange for your puppy's first veterinary examina-

tion beforehand, since many vets do not have appointments available immediately and your puppy should visit the vet within a day or so of coming home.

It's important to make sure your puppy's first visit to the vet is a pleasant and positive one. The vet should take great care to befriend the pup and handle him gently to make their first meeting a positive experience. The vet will give the pup a thorough physical examination and set up a schedule for vaccinations and other necessary wellness visits. Be sure to show your vet any health and inoculation records, which you should have received from your breeder. Your vet is a great source of canine health information, so be sure to ask questions and take notes. Creating a health journal for your puppy will make a handy reference for his wellness and any future health problems that may arise.

MEETING THE FAMILY

Your Kuvasz's homecoming is an exciting time for all members of the family, and it's only natural that everyone will be eager to meet him, pet him and play with him. However, for the puppy's sake, it's best to make these initial family meetings as uneventful as possible so that the pup is not overwhelmed with too much too soon. Remember, he has just left his dam and his littermates and is

away from the breeder's home for the first time. Despite his fuzzy wagging tail, he is still apprehensive and wondering where he is and who all these strange humans are. It's best to let him explore on his own and meet the family members as he feels comfortable. Let him investigate all the new smells, sights and sounds at his own pace. Children should be especially careful to not get overly excited, use loud voices or hug the pup too tightly. Be calm, gentle and affectionate, and be ready to comfort him if he appears frightened or uneasy.

Be sure to show your puppy his new crate during this first day home. Toss a treat or two inside the crate; if he associates the crate with food, he will associate the crate with good things. If he is comfortable with the crate, you can offer him his first meal inside it. Leave the door ajar so he can wander in and out as he chooses.

Start out on the right "paw" with your vet, and develop good communication with him, as he will care for your dogs' health throughout their entire lives.

THE CRITICAL SOCIALIZATION PERIOD

Canine research has shown that a puppy's 8th through 16th week is the most critical learning period of his life. This is when the puppy "learns to learn," a time when he needs positive experiences to build confidence and stability. Puppies who are not exposed to different people and situations outside the home during this period can grow up to be fearful and sometimes aggressive. This is also the best time for puppy lessons, since he has not yet acquired any bad habits that could undermine his ability to learn.

FIRST NIGHT IN HIS NEW HOME

So much has happened in your Kuvasz puppy's first day away from the breeder. He's had his first car ride to his new home. He's met his new human family and perhaps the other family pets. He has explored his new house and yard, at least those places where he is to be allowed during his first weeks at home. He may have visited his new veterinarian. He has eaten his first meal or two away from his dam and litter-mates. Surely that's enough to tire out an eight-week-old Kuvasz pup—or so you hope!

It's bedtime. During the day, the pup investigated his crate, which is his new den and sleeping space, so it is not entirely strange to him. Line the crate with a soft towel or blanket that he can snuggle into and gently place him into the crate for the night. Some breeders send home a piece of bedding from where the pup slept with his littermates, and those familiar scents are a great comfort for the puppy on his first night without his siblings.

He will probably whine or cry. The puppy is objecting to the confinement and the fact that he is alone for the first time. This can be a stressful time for you as well as for the pup. It's important that you remain strong and don't let the puppy out of his crate to comfort him. He will fall asleep eventually. If you release him, the puppy will learn that crying means "out" and will continue that habit. You are laying the groundwork for future habits. Some breeders find that soft music can soothe a crying pup and help him get to sleep.

SOCIALIZING YOUR PUPPY

The first 20 weeks of your Kuvasz puppy's life are the most important of his entire lifetime. A properly socialized puppy will grow up to be a confident and stable adult who will be a pleasure to live with and a welcome addition to the neighborhood.

The importance of socialization in the Kuvasz breed cannot be overemphasized. Research on canine behavior has proven that puppies who are not exposed to new sights, sounds, people and animals during their first 20 weeks of life will grow up to be timid and fearful, even aggressive, and unable to flourish outside of their home environment. This is even more true with the Kuvasz, a breed that is naturally protective and aloof with strangers.

Socializing your puppy is not difficult and, in fact, will be a fun time for you both. Lead training goes hand in hand with socialization, so your puppy will be learning how to walk on a lead at the same time that he's meeting the neighborhood. Because the Kuvasz is such a terrific breed, everyone will enjoy meeting "the new kid on the block." Take him for short walks to the park and to other dog-friendly places where he will encounter new people. Just make sure that you supervise these meetings. If you introduce your pup to children, make sure

that they do not get too rough or encourage him to play too hard. An overzealous pup can often nip too hard, frightening the child and in turn making the puppy overly excited. A bad experience in puppyhood can impact a dog for life, so a pup that has a negative experience with a child may grow up to be shy or even aggressive around children.

Take your puppy along on your daily errands. Puppies are natural "people magnets," and most people who see your pup will want to pet him. All of these encounters will help to mold him into a confident adult dog. Likewise, you will soon feel like a confident, responsible dog owner, rightly proud of your mannerly, well-adjusted Kuvasz.

Be especially careful of your puppy's encounters and experiences during the eight-to-ten-week-old period, which is also called the "fear period." This is a

Your pup may be a bit timid upon arrival at his new home. Don't worry, allow him to adapt at his own pace, and he will quickly become one of the family.

serious imprinting period, and all contact during this time should be gentle and positive. A frightening or negative event could leave a permanent impression that could affect his future behavior if a similar situation arises.

Also make sure that your puppy has received his first and second rounds of vaccinations before you expose him to other dogs or bring him to places that other dogs may frequent. Avoid dog parks and other strange-dog areas until your vet assures you that your puppy is fully immunized and resistant to the diseases that can be passed between canines. Discuss safe early socialization with your breeder and vet, as some recommend socializing the puppy even before he has received all of his inoculations.

LEADER OF THE PUPPY'S PACK

Like other canines, your puppy needs an authority figure, someone he can look up to and regard as the leader of his "pack." His first pack leader was his dam, who taught him to be polite and not chew too hard on her ears or nip at her muzzle. He learned those same lessons from his litter-mates. If he played too rough, they cried in pain and stopped the game, which sent an important message to the rowdy puppy.

As puppies play together, they are also struggling to determine

ESTABLISH A ROUTINE

Routine is very important to a puppy's learning environment. To facilitate house-training, use the same exit/entrance door for potty trips and always take the puppy to the same place in the yard. The same principle of consistency applies to all other aspects of puppy training.

who will be the boss. Being pack animals, dogs need someone to be in charge. If a litter of puppies remained together beyond puppyhood, one of the pups would emerge as the strongest one, the one who calls the shots.

Once your puppy leaves the pack, he will look intuitively for a new leader. If he does not recognize you as that leader, he will try to assume that position for himself. The Kuvasz is a natural leader and will vie for the position of "top dog" if he does not respect you as pack leader. You must remember that these are his natural canine instincts. Do not cave in and allow your pup to get the upper "paw."

Just as socialization is so important during these first 20 weeks, so too is your puppy's early education. He was born without any bad habits. He does not know what is good or bad behavior. If he does things like nipping and digging, it's because he is having fun and doesn't know that humans consider these things as "bad." It's your job to teach him proper puppy manners, and this is the best time to accomplish that—before he has developed bad habits, since it is much more difficult to "unlearn" or correct unacceptable learned behavior than to teach good behavior from the start.

Make sure that all members of the family understand the importance of being consistent when training their new puppy. For example, a good way to reinforce your role as leader is to not allow your youngster to get on the furniture. This is a privilege that can be given later, but only when you allow it. If your daughter allows your pup to cuddle on the couch to watch her

The excursion from the breeder's kennel to your home is a tiring one for pups. Try not to overwhelm him with too much once he comes home.

favorite television show with her, your pup will be confused about what he is and is not allowed to do. Have a family conference before your pup comes home so that everyone understands the basic principles of puppy training and the rules you have set forth for the pup and agrees to follow them.

The old saying that "an ounce

Your Kuvasz learned early life lessons from the rest of his pack. It is up to you, his new "pack" leader, to teach the pup how to be an acceptable member of canine society.

of prevention is worth a pound of cure" is especially true when it comes to puppies. It is much easier to prevent inappropriate behavior than it is to change it. It's also easier and less stressful for the pup, since it will keep discipline to a minimum and create a more positive learning environment for him. That, in turn, will also be easier on you.

Here are a few commonsense tips to keep your belongings safe and your puppy out of trouble:

- Keep your closet doors closed and your shoes, socks and other apparel off the floor so your puppy can't get to them.
- Keep a secure lid on the trash container or put the trash where your puppy can't dig into it. He can't damage what he can't reach!
- Supervise your puppy at all

BE CONSISTENT
Consistency is a key element, in fact is absolutely necessary, to a puppy's learning environment. A behavior (such as chewing, jumping up or climbing onto the furniture) cannot be forbidden one day and then allowed the next. That will only confuse the pup, and he will not understand what he is supposed to do. Just one or two episodes of allowing an undesirable behavior to "slide" will imprint that behavior on a puppy's brain and make that behavior more difficult to erase or change.

times to make sure he is not getting into mischief. If he starts to chew the corner of the rug, you can distract him instantly by tossing a toy for him to fetch. You also will be able to whisk him outside when you notice that he is about to piddle on the carpet. If you can't see your puppy, you can't teach him or correct his behavior.

SOLVING PUPPY PROBLEMS

CHEWING AND NIPPING
Nipping at fingers and toes is normal puppy behavior. Chewing is also the way that puppies investigate their surroundings. However, you will have to teach your puppy that chewing anything other than his toys is not acceptable. That won't happen overnight and at times puppy teeth will test your patience. However, if you allow nipping and chewing to continue, just think about the damage that a mature Kuvasz can do with a full set of adult teeth.

Whenever your puppy nips your hand or fingers, cry out "Ouch!" in a loud voice, which should startle your puppy and stop him from nipping, even if only for a moment. Immediately distract him by offering a small treat or an appropriate toy for him to chew instead (which means having chew toys and puppy treats handy or in your pockets at all times). Praise him when he takes the toy and tell him what a good fellow he is. Praise is just as or even more important in puppy training as discipline and correction. Stopping your pup's nipping is not only teaching him good behavior but also teaching him his place in the pack.

Puppies also tend to nip at children more often than adults, since they perceive little ones to be more vulnerable and more similar to their littermates. Teach your children appropriate responses to nipping behavior. If they are unable to handle it themselves, you may have to intervene. Puppy nips can be quite painful and a child's frightened reaction will only encourage a puppy to nip harder, which is a natural canine response. As with all other puppy situations, interaction between your Kuvasz puppy and children should be supervised.

Chewing on objects, not just family members' fingers and ankles, is also normal canine behavior that can be especially tedious (for the owner, not the pup) during the teething period when the puppy's adult teeth are coming in. At this stage, chewing just plain feels good. Furniture legs and cabinet corners are common puppy favorites. Shoes and other personal items also taste pretty good to a pup.

The best solution is, once again, prevention. If you value something, keep it tucked away and out of reach. You can't hide

your dining-room table in a closet, but you can try to deflect the chewing by applying a bitter product made just to deter dogs from chewing. This spray-on substance is vile-tasting, although safe for dogs, and most puppies will avoid the forbidden object after one tiny taste. You also can apply the product to your leather leash if the puppy tries to chew on his lead during leash-training sessions.

Keep a ready supply of safe chews handy to offer your Kuvasz as a distraction when he starts to chew on something that's a "no-no." Remember, at this tender age he does not yet know what is permitted or forbidden, so you have to be "on call" every minute

A nipping Kuvasz can be annoying. Nip this behavior in the bud as soon as it rears its ugly head.

he's awake and on the prowl.

You may lose a treasure or two during puppy's growing-up period, and the furniture could sustain a nasty nick or two. These can be trying times, so be prepared for those inevitable accidents and comfort yourself in knowing that this too shall pass.

JUMPING UP

Puppies jump up—on you, your guests, your counters and your furniture. Just another normal part of growing up, and one you need to meet head-on before it becomes an ingrained habit and you have 100 pounds of Kuvasz flying at you in an exuberant greeting.

The key to jump correction is consistency. You cannot correct your Kuvasz for jumping up on you today, then allow it to happen tomorrow by greeting him with hugs and kisses. As you have learned by now, consistency is critical to all puppy lessons.

For starters, try turning your back as soon as the puppy jumps. Jumping up is a means of gaining your attention and, if the pup can't see your face, he may get discouraged and learn that he loses eye contact with his beloved master when he jumps up.

Leash corrections also work, and most puppies respond well to a leash tug if they jump. Grasp the leash close to the puppy's collar and give a quick tug downward, using the command "Off." Do not use the word "Down," since "Down" is used to teach the puppy to lie down, which is a separate action that he will learn during his education in the basic commands. As soon as the puppy has backed off, tell him to sit and immediately praise him for doing so. This will take many repetitions and won't be accomplished quickly, so don't get discouraged or give up; you must be even more persistent than your puppy.

A second method used for jump correction is the spritzer bottle. Fill a spray bottle with water mixed with a bit of lemon juice or vinegar. As soon as the puppy jumps, command him "Off" and spritz him with the water mixture. Of course, that

TEETHING TIME

All puppies chew. It's normal canine behavior. Chewing just plain feels good to a puppy, especially during the three- to five-month teething period when the adult teeth are breaking through the gums. Rather than attempting to eliminate such a strong natural chewing instinct, you will be more successful if you redirect it and teach your puppy what he may or may not chew. Correct inappropriate chewing with a sharp "No!" and offer him a chew toy, praising him when he takes it. Don't become discouraged. Chewing usually decreases after the adult teeth have come in.

DIGGING OUT

Some dogs love to dig. Others wouldn't think of it. Digging is considered "self-rewarding behavior" because it's fun! Of all the digging solutions offered by the experts, most are only marginally successful and none is guaranteed to work. The best cure is prevention, which means removing the dog from the offending site when he digs as well as distracting him when you catch him digging so that he turns his attentions elsewhere. That means that you have to supervise your dog's yard time. An unsupervised digger can create havoc with your landscaping or, worse, run away!

Important to prevention is also knowing what you should not do. Never kick your Kuvasz (for any reason, not just for jumping) or knock him in the chest with your knee. That maneuver could actually harm your puppy. Vets can tell you stories about puppies who suffered broken bones after being banged about when they jumped up.

PUPPY WHINING

Puppies often cry and whine, just as infants and little children do. It's their way of telling us that they are lonely or in need of attention. Your puppy will miss his littermates and will feel insecure when he is left alone.

means having the spray bottle handy whenever or wherever jumping usually happens.

Yet a third method to discourage jumping is grasping the puppy's paws and holding them gently but firmly until he struggles to get away. Wait a brief moment or two, then release his paws and give him a command to sit. He should eventually learn that jumping gets him into an uncomfortable predicament.

Children are major victims of puppy jumping, since puppies view little people as ready targets for jumping up as well as nipping. If your children (or their friends) are unable to dispense jump corrections, you will have to intervene and handle it for them.

The time to teach proper canine behavior is now! Don't allow your Kuvasz puppy to jump up on you if you don't want him to continue doing so as an adult.

You may be out of the house or just in another room, but he will still feel alone. During these times, the puppy's crate should be his personal comfort station, a place all his own where he can feel safe and secure. Once he learns that being alone is okay and not something to be feared, he will settle down without crying or objecting. You might want to leave a radio on while he is crated, as the sound of human voices can be soothing and will give the impression that people are around.

Give your puppy a favorite cuddly toy or chew toy to entertain him whenever he is crated. You will both be happier:

"People food" can upset your Kuvasz's diet, add excess weight and even cause him serious injury, so be sure to keep such tantalizing treats out of his reach.

the puppy because he is safe in his den and you because he is quiet, safe and not getting into puppy escapades that can wreak havoc in your house or cause him danger.

To make sure that your puppy will always view his crate as a safe and cozy place, never, ever use the crate as punishment. That's the best way to turn the crate into a negative place that the pup will want to avoid. Sure, you can use the crate for your own peace of mind if your puppy is getting into trouble and needs some "time out." Just don't let him know that. Never scold the pup and immediately place him into the crate. Count to ten, give him a couple of hugs and maybe a treat, then scoot him into his crate.

It's also important not to make a big fuss when he is released from the crate. That will make getting out of the crate more appealing than being in the crate, which is just the opposite of what you are trying to achieve.

COUNTER SURFING
What we like to call "counter surfing" is a normal extension of jumping and usually starts to happen as soon as a puppy realizes that he is big enough to stand on his hind legs and investigate the good stuff on the kitchen counter or the coffee table. Once again, you have to be there to

prevent it. As soon as you see your Kuvasz even start to raise himself up, startle him with a sharp "No!" or "Aaahh, aaahh!" If he succeeds and manages to get one or both paws on the forbidden surface, smack those paws (firmly but gently) and tell him "Off!" As soon as he's back on all four paws, command him to sit and praise at once.

For surf prevention, make sure to keep any edibles put away and well out of reach, where your Kuvasz can't see or smell them. It's the old rule of prevention yet again.

FOOD GUARDING

Some dogs are picky eaters; others approach every meal with enthusiasm. Occasionally, the true "chow hound" will become protective of his food, which is one dangerous step toward other aggressive behavior. Food guarding is obvious: your puppy will growl, snarl or even attempt to bite you if you approach his food bowl or put your hand into his pan while he's eating.

This behavior is not acceptable and is very preventable. If your puppy is an especially voracious eater, sit next to him occasionally while he eats and dangle your fingers in his food bowl. Eating too quickly is not healthy for him either, thought of as a possible cause of bloat, so his wolfing down his food should be

Welcoming a Kuvasz puppy into your life is an exciting and joyous occasion.

prevented regardless. Don't feed him in a corner, where he could feel possessive of his eating space. Rather, place his food bowl in an open area of your kitchen where you are in close proximity. Occasionally remove his food in mid-meal, tell him he's a good boy and return his bowl.

If your pup becomes possessive of his food, look for other signs of future aggression, like guarding his favorite toys or refusing to obey obedience commands that he knows. Consult an obedience trainer for help in reinforcing obedience so your Kuvasz will fully understand that you are the boss.

PROPER CARE OF YOUR

KUVASZ

Adding a Kuvasz to your household means adding a new family member who will need your care each and every day. When your Kuvasz pup first comes home, you will start a routine with him so that, as he grows up, your dog will have a daily schedule just as you do. The aspects of your dog's daily care will likewise become regular parts of your day, so you'll both have a new schedule. Dogs learn by consistency and thrive on routine: regular times for meals, exercise, grooming and potty trips are just as important for your dog as they are for you. Your dog's schedule will depend much on your family's daily routine, but remember that you now have a new member of the family who is part of your day every day.

Your Kuvasz's first caregivers were his parents, as demonstrated here by Markie and a young pup, owner Sue Thomas. It is now your turn to take over as provider.

FEEDING THE KUVASZ

Feeding your dog the best diet is based on various factors, including age, activity level, overall condition and size of breed. When you visit the breeder, he will share with you his advice about the proper diet for your dog based on his experience with the breed and the foods with which he has had success. Likewise, your vet will be a helpful source of advice throughout the dog's life and will aid you in planning a diet for optimal health.

Historically, the Kuvasz spent a lot of time on its own guarding livestock. During this time, the dogs ate irregularly and lived on an inconsistent diet of question-able nutritional value. That shouldn't be the case for the breed today. A premium dog food, one found in specialty stores, will do for the Kuvasz. Some dog-food companies make specific foods especially for working dogs. However, many fanciers recommend a natural or

Pups are introduced to solid foods as part of the weaning process.

homemade diet. Consult your veterinarian or breeder for more information on what they feel is best for the breed.

Fruit (except grapes) and vegetables make great snacks and playthings for the Kuvasz. Commercially prepared treats are okay, as long as they are free of dyes and additives. Vitamin supplements are unnecessary because this breed very effectively processes its meals, a result of being a working dog that spent many days in the field with the livestock.

NO-FRILLS DIET

The Kuvasz doesn't need a high-protein food or vitamin supplements. The breed processes its food very effectively, just as a working dog that protects livestock should. Historically, out in the field this breed would not have been fed the rich diets available on the market today.

FEEDING THE PUPPY

Of course, your pup's very first food will be his dam's milk. There may be special situations in which pups fail to nurse, necessi-tating that the breeder hand-feed them with a formula, but for the most part pups spend the first weeks of life nursing from their dam. The breeder weans the pups

SWITCHING FOODS

There are certain times in a dog's life when it becomes necessary to switch his food; for example, from puppy to adult food and then from adult to senior-dog food. Additionally, you may decide to feed your pup a different type of food from what he received from the breeder, and there may be "emergency" situations in which you can't find your dog's normal brand and have to offer something else temporarily. Anytime a change is made, for whatever reason, the switch must be done gradually. You don't want to upset the dog's stomach or end up with a picky eater who refuses to eat something new. A tried-and-true approach is, over the course of about a week, to mix a little of the new food in with the old, increasing the proportion of new to old as the days progress. At the end of the week, you'll be feeding his regular portions of the new food, and he will barely notice the change.

by gradually introducing solid foods and decreasing the milk meals. Pups may even start themselves off on the weaning process, albeit inadvertently, if they snatch bites from their mom's food bowl.

By the time the pups are ready for new homes, they are fully weaned and eating a good puppy food. As a new owner, you may be thinking, "Great! The breeder has taken care of the hard part." Not so fast.

A puppy's first year of life is the time when most of his growth and development takes place. This is a delicate time, especially for a large-breed pup, and diet plays a huge role in proper skeletal and muscular formation. Improper diet and exercise habits can lead to damaging problems that will compromise the dog's health and movement for his entire life. That being said, new owners should not worry needlessly. With the myriad types of food formulated specifically for growing pups of different-sized breeds, dog-food manufacturers have taken much of the guesswork out of feeding your puppy well. A Kuvasz puppy should not have too much protein, which can cause the puppy to grow too quickly, resulting in poorly formed joints and other problems. Foods labeled for large breeds are best for this reason.

Since puppy-food formulas are designed to provide the nutrition that a growing puppy needs, it is unnecessary and, in fact, can prove harmful to add supplements to the diet, as too much of certain vitamin supplements and minerals predispose a dog to skeletal problems. It's by no means a case of "if a little is good, a lot is better." At every stage of your dog's life, too much or too little in the way of nutrients can be harmful, which is why a manufactured complete food is the easiest way to know that your dog is getting what he needs.

Because of a young pup's small body and accordingly small digestive system, his daily portion will be divided up into small meals throughout the day. This can mean starting off with three or more meals a day and decreasing the number of meals as the pup matures. For the adult Kuvasz, the day's food should be divided into two meals on a morning/evening schedule rather than offered in one large portion, as this is healthier for the dog's digestion and will reduce the risk of the deadly gastric torsion (bloat).

Regarding the feeding schedule, feeding the pup at the same times and in the same place each day is important for both housebreaking purposes and establishing the dog's everyday routine. Further, Kuvaszok of any age should be given plenty of quiet time before and after meals, so plan his exercise sessions at least one hour before and two hours after mealtimes.

As for the amount to feed, growing puppies generally need proportionately more food per body weight than their adult counterparts, but a pup should never be allowed to gain excess weight. Dogs of all ages should be kept in proper body condition, but extra weight can strain a pup's developing frame, causing skeletal problems. Consult your veterinarian for the proper amount to feed a pup.

Watch your pup's weight as he grows and, if the recommended amounts seem to be too much or too little for your pup, consult the vet about appropriate dietary changes. Keep in mind that treats, although small, can quickly add up throughout the day, contributing unnecessary calories. Treats are fine when used prudently; opt for dog treats specially formulated to be healthy or for nutritious snacks like small pieces of cheese or cooked chicken.

A balanced diet will keep your Kuvasz fit and healthy, not to mention extremely happy.

What Is "Bloat" and How Do I Prevent it?

You likely have heard the term "bloat," which refers to gastric torsion (gastric dilatation/volvulus), a potentially fatal condition. It is directly related to feeding and exercise practices, and a brief explanation here is warranted. The term *dilatation* means that the dog's stomach is filled with air, while *volvulus* means that the stomach is twisted around on itself, blocking the entrance/exit points. Dilatation/volvulus is truly a deadly combination, although they also can occur independently of each other. An affected dog cannot digest food or pass gas, and blood cannot flow to the stomach, causing accumulation of toxins and gas along with great pain and rapidly occuring shock.

Many theories exist on what exactly causes bloat, but we do know that deep-chested breeds are more prone. Activities like eating a large meal, gulping water, strenuous exercise too close to mealtimes or a combination of these factors can contribute to bloat, though not every case is directly related to these more well-known causes. With that in mind, we can focus on incorporating simple daily preventives and knowing how to recognize the symptoms. In addition to the tips presented in this book, ask your vet about how to prevent and recognize bloat. An affected dog needs immediate veterinary attention, as death can result quickly. Signs include obvious restlessness/discomfort, crying in pain, drooling/excessive salivation, unproductive attempts to vomit or relieve himself, visibly bloated appearance and collapsing. Do not wait: get to the vet *right away* if you see any of these symptoms. The vet will confirm by x-ray if the stomach is bloated with air; if so, the dog must be treated *immediately*.

As varied as the causes of bloat are the tips for prevention, but some common preventive methods follow:
• Feed two or three small meals daily rather than one large one;
• Do not feed water before, after or with meals, but allow access to water at all other times;
• Never permit rapid eating or gulping of water;
• No exercise for the dog at least two hours before and (especially) after meals;
• Feed high-quality food with adequate protein, adequate fiber content and not too much fat and carbohydrate;
• Explore herbal additives, enzymes or gas-reduction products (only under a vet's advice) to encourage a "friendly" environment in the dog's digestive system;
• Avoid foods and ingredients known to produce gas;
• Avoid stressful situations for the dog, especially at mealtimes;
• Make dietary changes gradually, over a period of a few weeks;
• Do not feed dry food only;
• Although the role of genetics as a causative of bloat is not known, many breeders do not breed from previously affected dogs;
• Sometimes owners are advised to have gastroplexy (stomach stapling) performed on their dogs as a preventive measure.
Pay attention to your dog's behavior and any changes that could be symptomatic of bloat. Your dog's life depends on it!

FEEDING THE ADULT DOG

For the adult (meaning physically mature) dog, feeding properly is about maintenance, not growth. The Kuvasz continues to mature until past two years of age, so ask your breeder and vet about the appropriate age to switch to an adult-formula food. Again, correct weight is a concern. Your dog should appear fit and should have an evident "waist." His ribs should not be protruding (a sign of being underweight), but they should be covered by only a slight layer of fat. The Kuvasz should never be overweight, which will put undue strain on his joints. Because this is a heavily coated breed, it's often difficult to tell if an individual has gained weight—unless, of course, the dog has lost his waist and becomes roly-poly. Your veterinarian will help you determine the healthy weight range for your dog. You should evaluate your Kuvasz's condition regularly with a hands-on check to feel under the coat, rather than just by sight.

Under normal circumstances, an adult Kuvasz can be maintained fairly easily with a high-quality nutritionally complete adult-formula food. Factor treats into your dog's overall daily caloric intake, and avoid offering table scraps. Not only are certain "people foods," like chocolate, nuts, raisins, grapes, onions and significant quantities of garlic, toxic to dogs but feeding from your plate also encourages begging and overeating. Overweight dogs are more prone to health problems. Research has even shown that obesity takes years off a dog's life. With that in mind, resist the urge to overfeed and over-treat. Don't make unnecessary additions to your dog's diet, whether with tidbits or with extra vitamins and minerals.

THE DARK SIDE OF CHOCOLATE

From a tiny chip to a giant rabbit, chocolate—in any form—is not your dog's friend. Whether it's an Oreo® cookie, a Snickers® bar or even a couple of M&M's®, you should avoid these items with your dog. You are also well advised to avoid any bone toy that is made out of fake chocolate or any treat made of carob—anything that encourages your dog to become a "chocoholic" can't be helpful. Before you toss your pooch half of your candy bar, consider that as little as a single ounce of chocolate can poison a 30-pound dog. Theobromine, like caffeine, is a methylxanthine and occurs naturally in cocoa beans. Dogs metabolize theobromine very slowly, and its effect on the dog can be serious, harming the heart, kidneys and central nervous system. Dark or semi-sweet chocolate is even worse than milk chocolate, and baking chocolate and cocoa mix are by far the worst.

The amount of food needed for proper maintenance will vary depending on the individual dog's activity level, but you will be able to tell whether the daily portions are keeping him in good shape. With the wide variety of good complete foods available, choosing what to feed is largely a matter of personal preference. Just as with the puppy, the adult dog should have consistency in his mealtimes and feeding place. In addition to a consistent routine, regular mealtimes allow you to practice the important daily bloat preventives related to feeding and exercise. You will also be able to see how much your dog is eating.

NOT HUNGRY?

No dog in his right mind would turn down his dinner, would he? If you notice that your dog has lost interest in his food, there could be any number of causes. Dental problems are a common cause of appetite loss, one that is often overlooked. If your dog has a toothache, a loose tooth or sore gums from infection, chances are it doesn't feel so good to chew. Think about when you've had a toothache! If your dog does not approach the food bowl with his usual enthusiasm, look inside his mouth for signs of a problem. Whatever the cause, you'll want to consult your vet so that your chow hound can get back to his happy, hungry self as soon as possible.

If the dog seems never to be satisfied or, likewise, becomes uninterested in his food, you will know right away that something is wrong and can consult your veterinarian.

DIETS FOR THE AGING DOG

A good rule of thumb is that once a dog has reached 75% of his expected lifespan, he has reached "senior citizen" or geriatric status. Your Kuvasz will be considered a senior at about seven years of age; he has a projected lifespan of ten years and over. The smallest breeds generally enjoy the longest lives and the largest breeds the shortest, but the Kuvasz is a generally healthy breed that has been known to live to 14 years old, sometimes even longer.

What does aging have to do with your dog's diet? No, he won't get a discount at the local diner's early-bird special. Yes, he will require some dietary changes to accommodate the changes that come along with increased age. One change is that the older dog's dietary needs become more similar to those of a puppy. Specifically, dogs can metabolize more protein as youngsters and seniors than in the adult-maintenance stage. Discuss with your vet whether you need to switch to a higher-protein or senior-formulated food or whether your current adult-dog food contains sufficient nutrition for the senior.

Watching the dog's weight remains essential, even more so in the senior stage. Older dogs are already more vulnerable to illness, and obesity only contributes to their susceptibility to problems. As the older dog becomes less active and thus exercises less, his regular portions may cause him to gain weight. At this point, you may consider decreasing his daily food intake or switching to a reduced-calorie food. As with other changes, you should consult your vet for advice.

TYPES OF FOOD AND READING THE LABEL

When selecting the type of food to feed your dog, it is important to check out the label for ingredients. Many dry-food products have soybean, corn or rice as the main ingredient. The main ingredient will be listed first on the label, with the rest of the ingredients following in descending order according to their proportion in the food. While these types of dry food are fine, you should look into dry foods based on meat or fish. These are better-quality foods and thus higher priced. However, they may be just as economical in the long run, because studies have shown that it takes less of the higher-quality foods to maintain a dog.

Comparing the various types of food, dry, canned and semi-moist, dry foods contain the least

You are what you eat! The same is true for your Kuvasz. Feed a diet recommended by your veterinarian or breeder.

amount of water and canned foods the most. Proportionately, dry foods are the most calorie- and nutrient-dense, which means that you need more of a canned food product to supply the same amount of nutrition. In households with breeds of different sizes, the canned/dry/semi-moist question can be of special importance. Larger breeds obviously eat more than smaller ones and thus in general do better on dry foods, but smaller breeds do fine on canned foods and require "small-bite" formulations to protect their small mouths and teeth if fed only dry foods. So if you have different-sized dogs in your home, consider both your own preferences and

QUENCHING HIS THIRST

Is your dog drinking more than normal and trying to lap up everything in sight? Excessive drinking has many different causes. Obvious causes for a dog's being thirstier than usual are hot weather and vigorous exercise. However, if your dog is drinking more for no apparent reason, you could have cause for concern. Serious conditions like kidney or liver disease, diabetes and various types of hormonal problems can all be indicated by excessive drinking. If you notice your dog's being excessively thirsty, contact your vet at once. Hopefully there will be a simpler explanation, but the earlier a serious problem is detected, the sooner it can be treated, with a better rate of cure.

what your dogs like to eat, but generally think canned for the little guys and dry or semi-moist for everyone else. You may find success mixing the food types as well. Water is important for all dogs but even more so for those fed dry foods, as there is no high water content in their food.

There are strict controls that regulate the nutritional content of dog food, and a food has to meet the minimum requirements in order to be considered "complete and balanced." It is important that you choose such a food for your dog, so check the label to be sure that your chosen food meets the requirements. If not, look for a food that clearly states on the label that it is formulated to be complete and balanced for your dog's particular stage of life.

Recommendations for amounts to feed will also be indicated on the label. You should also ask your vet about proper food portions, and you will keep an eye on your dog's condition to see whether the recommended amounts are adequate. If he becomes over- or underweight, you will need to make adjustments; this also would be a good time to consult your vet.

The food label may also make feeding suggestions, such as whether moistening a dry-food product is recommended. Sometimes a splash of water will make the food more palatable for the dog and even enhance the flavor. A bit of water in a dry-food product is recommended for Kuvaszok to slow down their eating as a bloat preventive. Don't be overwhelmed by the many factors that go into feeding your dog. Manufacturers of complete and balanced foods make it easy, and once you find the right food and amounts for your Kuvasz, his daily feeding will be a matter of routine.

DON'T FORGET THE WATER!
Regardless of what type of food your Kuvasz eats, there's no doubt that he needs plenty of water.

Fresh cold water, in a clean bowl, should be freely available to your dog. There are special circumstances, such as during puppy housebreaking, when you will want to monitor your pup's water intake so that you will be able to predict when he will need to relieve himself, but water must be available to him nonetheless. Water is essential for hydration and proper body function just as it is in humans.

You will get to know how much your dog typically drinks in a day. Of course, in the heat or if exercising vigorously, he will be more thirsty and will drink more. However, if he begins to drink noticeably more water for no apparent reason, this could signal any of various problems, and you are advised to consult your vet.

A word of caution concerning your deep-chested dog's water intake: he should never be allowed to gulp water, especially at mealtimes. In fact, his water intake should be limited to a few licks at mealtimes as a rule. This simple daily precaution can go a long way in protecting your dog from the dangerous and potentially fatal gastric torsion (bloat).

EXERCISE
We all know the importance of exercise for humans, so it should come as no surprise that it is essential for our canine friends as well. Now, regardless of your own level of fitness, get ready to assume the role of personal

The Kuvasz is no fair-weather friend, and he will be happy to stretch his legs no matter what the weather.

trainer for your dog. It's not as hard as it sounds, and it will have health benefits for you, too.

Just as with anything else you do with your dog, you must set a routine for his exercise. It's the same as your daily morning run before work or never missing the 7 P.M. aerobics class. If you plan it and get into the habit of actually doing it, it will become just another part of your day. Think of it as making daily exercise appointments with your dog, and stick to your schedule.

As a rule, Kuvaszok in normal health should have at least two half-hour sessions of activity each day. Dogs with health or orthopedic problems may have specific limitations, so their exercise plans are best devised with the help of a vet. For healthy dogs, there are many ways to fit this activity into your day. Depending on your schedule, you

Proper nutrition and adequate exercise will be evident in your Kuvasz's overall good condition.

> ## PUPPY STEPS
> Puppies are brimming with activity and enthusiasm. It seems that they can play all day and night without tiring, but don't overdo your puppy's exercise regimen. Easy does it for the puppy's first 18 months. Keep walks brief and don't let the puppy engage in stressful jumping games. The puppy frame is delicate, and too much exercise during those critical growing months can cause injury to his bone structure, ligaments and musculature. Save his first jog for his first birthday!

may plan a 30-minute walk or activity session in the morning and again in the evening, or you may want to have an extra-long walk or playtime supplemented by a couple of shorter activity times, remembering to schedule all exercise well before or after mealtimes. Walking is the most popular way to exercise a dog (it's good for you, too!); other suggestions include retrieving games, disc-catching or other active games with his toys. If you have a safe body of water nearby, and a Kuvasz that likes to swim (not all Kuvaszok do!), swimming is an excellent form of exercise for dogs, putting no stress on his frame.

On that note, some precautions should be taken with a puppy's exercise. During his first 18 months, when he is doing most

Brushing the coat daily will stimulate the coat's natural oils, remove dead hair and prevent matting.

of his growing and developing, your Kuvasz should not be subject to vigorous activity that stresses his body. Short walks at a comfortable pace and play sessions in the yard are good for a growing pup, and his exercise can be increased as he grows up.

For overweight dogs, dietary changes and activity will help the goal of weight loss. (Sound familiar?) While they should of course be encouraged to be active, remember not to overdo it, as the excess weight is already putting strain on their vital organs and bones. As for highly active dogs, some of them never seem to tire! They will enjoy time spent with their owners doing things together.

Regardless of your dog's condition and activity level, exercise offers benefits to all dogs and owners. Consider the fact that dogs who are kept active are more stimulated both physically and mentally, meaning that they are less likely to become bored and lapse into destructive behavior. Also consider the benefits of one-on-one time with your dog every day, continually strengthening the bond between the two of you. Furthermore, exercising together will improve health and longevity for both of you. You both need exercise, and now you and your dog have a workout partner and motivator!

The Kuvasz does indeed shed and will shed even more than usual in warmer climates. Brush the dog a few times a week (every day if possible) to remove the loose hair and to prevent mats from forming; mats commonly form behind the Kuvasz's ears. While brushing, run your hands all over the dog to check for any unusual growths or other abnormalities that will easily be concealed by the coat. Twice a year, generally in the fall and spring, the Kuvasz will shed excessively ("blow his coat") as

Introduce the Kuvasz to grooming at a young age.

GROOMING

A heavily coated dog like the Kuvasz might appear to be rather difficult to keep clean and neatly groomed, but those who own the Kuvasz know that the coat basically takes care of itself. Despite all of that white hair, the Kuvasz does not get dirty easily. The texture of the hair is such that it does not take on water or dirt, keeping the Kuvasz white and without much doggy odor. Most dry dirt can be simply brushed out. Remember, this is a breed meant to spend most of its time outdoors with livestock, so the coat is meant to protect the dog from the elements.

WATER SHORTAGE

No matter how well behaved your dog is, bathing is always a project! Nothing can substitute for a good warm bath, but owners do have the option of giving their dogs "dry" baths. Pet shops sell excellent products, in both powder and spray forms, designed for spot-cleaning your dog. These dry shampoos are convenient for touch-up jobs when you don't have the time to bathe your dog in the traditional way.

Muddy feet, messy behinds and smelly coats can be spot-cleaned and deodorized with a "wet-nap"-style cleaner. On those days when your dog insists on rolling in fresh goose droppings and there's no time for a bath, a spot bath can save the day. These pre-moistened wipes are also handy for other grooming needs like wiping faces, ears and eyes and freshening tails and behinds.

the coat changes from its summer to winter version and back again. Brush the dog more frequently during this time.

BATHING

The Kuvasz needs to be washed only when truly necessary. Most fanciers caution against regular bathing, which will remove the dog's natural skin oils and ruin the coat's dirt-repelling qualities, and recommend bathing only about twice a year. Use a gentle shampoo made for dogs, something that will be easy on the dog's eyes if suds should wash into them. There are also special shampoos for white dogs that help them look whiter. Human shampoos are too harsh for dogs' coats and will dry them out.

If you give your dog his first bath when he is young, he will become accustomed to the process. Wrestling a dog into the tub or chasing a freshly shampooed dog who has escaped from the bath will be no fun! Most dogs don't naturally enjoy their baths, but you at least want yours to cooperate with you.

Before bathing the dog, have the items you'll need close at hand. First, decide where you will bathe the dog. You should have a tub or basin with a non-slip surface. Young puppies can even be bathed in a sink. In warm weather, some like to use a portable pool in the yard, although you'll want to make sure your dog doesn't head for the nearest dirt pile following his bath! You will also need a hose or shower spray to wet the coat thoroughly, your doggie-formula shampoo, absorbent towels and perhaps a blow dryer.

Before wetting the dog, give him a brush-through to remove any dead hair, dirt and mats. Make sure he is at ease in the tub and have the water at a comfortable temperature. Begin bathing by wetting the coat all the way down to the skin. Massage in the shampoo, keeping it away from his face and eyes. Rinse him

Grooming time will allow you to check your Kuvasz for skin conditions that might otherwise go unnoticed.

thoroughly, again avoiding the eyes and ears, as you don't want to get water into the ear canals. A thorough rinsing is important, as shampoo residue is drying and itchy to the dog. After rinsing, wrap him in a towel to absorb the initial moisture. You can finish drying with either a towel or a blow dryer on low heat, held at a safe distance from the dog. You should keep the dog indoors and away from drafts until he is completely dry.

NAIL CLIPPING

Having their nails trimmed is not on many dogs' lists of favorite things to do. With this in mind, you will need to accustom your puppy to the procedure at a young age so that he will sit still (well, as still as he can) for his pedicures. Long nails can cause the dog's feet to spread, which is

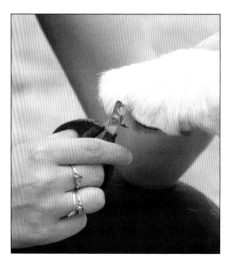

Heavy-duty canine nail clippers will be needed to clip your Kuvasz's nails at home.

THE MONTHLY GRIND

If your dog doesn't like the feeling of nail clippers or if you're not comfortable using them, you may wish to try an electric nail grinder. This tool has a small sandpaper disc on the end that rotates to grind the nails down. Some feel that using a grinder reduces the risk of cutting into the quick; this can be true if the tool is used properly. Usually you will be able to tell where the quick is before you get to it. A benefit of the grinder is that it creates a smooth finish on the nails so that there are no ragged edges.

Because the tool makes noise, your dog should be introduced to it before the actual grinding takes place. Turn it on and let your dog hear the noise; turn it off and let him inspect it with you holding it. Use the grinder gently, holding it firmly and progressing a little at a time until you reach the proper length. Look at the nail as you grind so that you do not go too short. Stop at any indication that you are nearing the quick. It will take a few sessions for both you and the puppy to get used to the grinder. Make sure that you don't let his hair get tangled in the grinder!

not good for him; likewise, long nails can hurt if they unintentionally scratch, not good for you.

Some dogs' nails are worn down naturally by regular walking on hard surfaces, so the frequency with which you clip depends on your individual dog. Look at his nails from time to time and clip as needed; a good way to know when it's time for a trim is if you hear your dog clicking as he walks across the floor.

There are several types of nail clippers and even electric nail-grinding tools made for dogs; first we'll discuss using the clipper. To start, have your clipper ready and some doggie treats on hand. You want your pup to view his nail-clipping sessions in a positive light, and what better way to convince him than with food? You may want to enlist the help of an assistant to comfort the pup and offer treats as you concentrate on the clipping itself. The guillotine-type clipper is thought of by many as the easiest type to use; the nail tip is inserted into the opening, and blades on the top and bottom snip it off in one clip.

Start by grasping the pup's paw; a little pressure on the foot pad causes the nail to extend, making it easier to clip. Clip off a little at a time. If you can see the "quick," which is a blood vessel that runs through each nail, you will know how much to trim, as you do not want to cut into the quick. On that note, if you do cut the quick, which will cause bleeding, you can stem the flow of blood with a styptic pencil or other clotting agent. If you mistakenly nip the quick, do not panic

By introducing your Kuvasz to a nail-clipping routine early in life, he will become accustomed to it and remain cooperative.

or fuss, as this will cause the pup to be afraid. Simply reassure the pup, stop the bleeding and move on to the next nail. Don't be discouraged; you will become a professional canine pedicurist with practice.

You may or may not be able to see the quick, so it's best to just clip off a small bit at a time. If you see a dark dot in the center of the nail, this is the quick and your cue to stop clipping. Tell the puppy he's a "good boy" and offer a piece of treat with each nail. You can also use nail-clipping time to examine the footpads, making sure that they are not dry and cracked and that nothing has become embedded in them.

The nail grinder, the other

Use a cloth or cotton ball to clean the ears. Avoid using a cotton swab, which could harm the inner ear.

THE EARS KNOW

Examining your puppy's ears helps ensure good internal health. The ears are the eyes to the dog's innards! Begin handling your puppy's ears when he's still young so that he doesn't protest every time you lift a flap or touch his ears. Yeast and bacteria are two of the culprits that you can detect by examining the ear. You will notice a strong, often foul, odor, debris, redness or some kind of discharge. All of these point to health problems that can worsen over time. Additionally, you are on the lookout for wax accumulation, ear mites and other tiny bothersome parasites and their even tinier droppings. You may have to pluck hair with tweezers in order to have a better view into the dog's ears, but this is painless if done carefully.

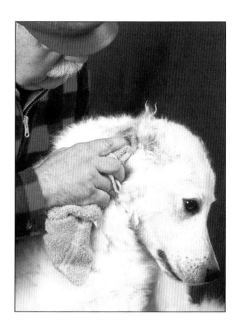

option, is many owners' first choice. Accustoming the puppy to the sound of the grinder and sensation of the buzz presents fewer challenges than the clipper, and there's no chance of cutting through the quick. Use the grinder on a low setting and always talk soothingly to your dog. He won't mind his salon visit, and he'll have nicely polished nails as well.

Ear Cleaning

While keeping your dog's ears clean unfortunately will not cause him to "hear" your commands any better, it will protect him from ear infection and ear-mite infestation. In addition, a dog's ears are vulnerable to waxy build-up and to collecting foreign matter from the

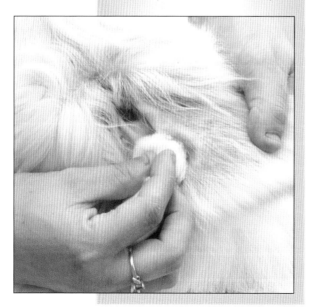

outdoors. Look in your dog's ears regularly to ensure that they look pink, clean and otherwise healthy, and check for a yeasty or foul odor. The Kuvaszok's flap-type ears don't allow for much air circulation. Even if they look fine, an odor in the ears signals a problem and means it's time to call the vet.

A dog's ears should be cleaned regularly; once a week is suggested, and you can do this along with your regular brushing. Using a cotton ball or pad and never probing into the ear canal, wipe the ear gently. You can use an ear-cleansing solution, available from your vet or pet-supply store; alternatively, you might prefer to use homemade solutions with ingredients like one part white vinegar and one part hydrogen peroxide. Ask your vet about home remedies before you attempt to concoct something on your own.

Keep your dog's ears free of excess hair by plucking it as needed. If done gently, this will be painless for the dog. Look for wax, brown droppings (a sign of ear mites), redness or any other abnormalities. At the first sign of a problem, contact your vet so that he can prescribe an appropriate medication.

EYE CARE

During grooming sessions, pay extra attention to the condition of your dog's eyes. If the area around the eyes is soiled or if tear staining has occurred, there are various cleaning agents made especially for this purpose. Look at the dog's

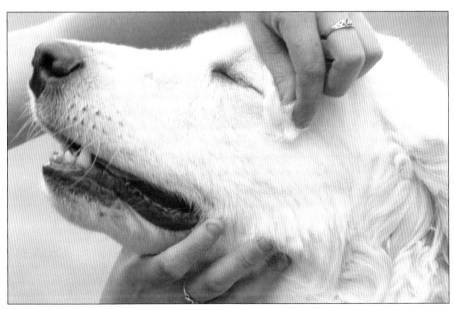

Wiping around the eyes with cotton and a specially made cleansing solution will remove tear stains from your Kuvasz's face.

eyes to make sure no debris has entered; dogs with large eyes and those who spend time outdoors are especially prone to this.

The signs of an eye infection are obvious: mucus, redness, puffiness, scabs or other signs of irritation. If your dog's eyes become infected, the vet will likely prescribe an antibiotic ointment for treatment. If you notice signs of more serious problems, such as opacities in the eye, which usually indicate cataracts, consult the vet at once. Taking time to pay attention to your dog's eyes will alert you in the early stages of any problem so that you can get your dog treatment as soon as possible. You could save your dog's sight!

A CLEAN SMILE

Another essential part of grooming is brushing your dog's teeth and checking his overall oral condition. Studies show that around 80% of dogs experience

dental problems by two years of age, and the percentage is higher in older dogs. Therefore it is highly likely that your dog will have trouble with his teeth and gums unless you are proactive with home dental care.

The most common dental problem in dogs is plaque build-up. If not treated, this causes gum disease, infection and resultant tooth loss. Bacteria from these infections spread throughout the body, affecting the vital organs. Do you need much more convincing to start brushing your dog's teeth? If so, take a good whiff of your dog's breath, and read on.

Fortunately, home dental care is rather easy and convenient for pet owners. Specially formulated canine toothpaste is easy to find. You should use one of these toothpastes, not a product for humans. Some doggie pastes are even available in flavors appealing to dogs. If your dog likes the flavor, he will tolerate the process better, making things much easier for you! Doggie toothbrushes come in different sizes and are designed to fit the contour of a canine mouth. Rubber fingertip brushes fit right on one of your fingers and have rubber nodes to clean the teeth and massage the gums. This may be easier to handle, as it is akin to rubbing your dog's teeth with your finger.

Brushing your dog's teeth is an essential facet of his proper healthcare. Many serious problems can stem from a lack of effective dental care.

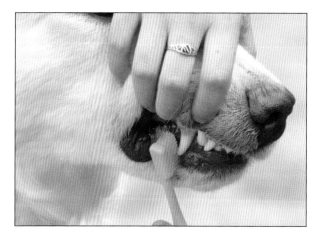

As with other grooming tasks, accustom your Kuvasz pup to his dental care early on. Start gently, for a few minutes at a time, so that he gets used to the feel of the brush and to your handling his mouth. Offer praise and petting so that he looks at tooth-care time as a time when he gets extra love and attention. The routine should become second nature; he may not like it, but he should at least tolerate it.

Aside from brushing, offer dental toys to your dog and feed crunchy biscuits, which help to minimize plaque. Rope toys have the added benefit of acting like floss as the dog chews. At your adult dog's yearly check-ups, the vet will likely perform a thorough tooth scraping as well as a complete check for any problems. These regular veterinary cleanings are also helpful to prevent tooth and gum damage due to bacterial growth. However, dogs are often anesthetized for veterinary tooth cleanings; since the Kuvasz is sensitive to anesthetic, make sure that your veterinarian understands this and treats the dog accordingly.

Proper care of your dog's teeth will ensure that you will enjoy your dog's smile for many years to come. The next time your dog goes to give you a hello kiss, you'll be glad you spent the time caring for his teeth.

SCOOTING HIS BOTTOM

Here's a doggy problem that many owners tend to neglect. If your dog is scooting his rear end around the carpet, he probably is experiencing anal-sac impaction or blockage. The anal sacs are the two grape-sized glands on either side of the dog's vent. The dog cannot empty these glands, which become filled with a foul-smelling material. The dog may attempt to lick the area to relieve the pressure. He may also rub his anus on your walls, furniture or floors.

Don't neglect your dog's rear end during grooming sessions. By squeezing both sides of the anus with a soft cloth, you can express some of the material in the sacs. If the material is pasty and thick, you likely will need the assistance of a veterinarian. Vets know how to express the glands and can show you how to do it correctly without hurting the dog or spraying yourself with the unpleasant liquid.

THE OTHER END
Dogs sometime have trouble with their anal glands, which are sacs located beside the anal vent. These should empty when a dog has normal bowel movements; if they don't, they can become full or impacted, causing discomfort. Owners often are alarmed to see their dogs scooting across the floor, dragging their behinds behind; this is just a dog's attempt

to empty the glands himself.

Some brave owners attempt to evacuate their dogs' anal glands themselves during grooming, but no one will tell you that this is a pleasant task. Thus many owners prefer to make the trip to the vet to have the vet take care of the problem; owners whose dogs visit a groomer can have this done by the groomer if he offers this as part of his services. Regardless, don't neglect the dog's other end in your home-care routine. Look for scooting, licking or other signs of discomfort "back there" to ascertain whether the anal glands need to be emptied.

IDENTIFICATION FOR YOUR DOG

You love your Kuvasz and want to keep him safe. Of course you take every precaution to prevent his escaping from the yard or becoming lost or stolen. You have a sturdy high fence and you always keep your dog on lead when out and about in public places. If your dog is not properly identified, however, you are overlooking a major aspect of his safety. We hope to never be in a situation where our dog is missing, but we should practice prevention in the unfortunate case that this happens; identification greatly increases the chances of your dog's being returned to you.

There are several ways to identify your dog. First, the traditional dog tag should be a staple in your dog's wardrobe, attached to his everyday collar. Tags can be made of sturdy plastic and various metals and should include your contact information so that a person who finds the dog can get in touch with you right away to arrange his return. Many people today enjoy the wide range of decorative tags available, so have fun and create a tag to match your dog's personality. Of course, it is important that the tag stays on the collar, so have a secure "O" ring attachment; you also can explore the type of tag that slides right onto the collar.

In addition to the ID tag, which every dog should wear even if identified by another method, two other forms of identification have become popular: microchipping and tattooing. In microchipping, a tiny scannable chip is painlessly inserted under the dog's skin. The number is

One method of permanent dog identification is tattooing. The tattoo should be placed in an easily visible area such as the inner ear.

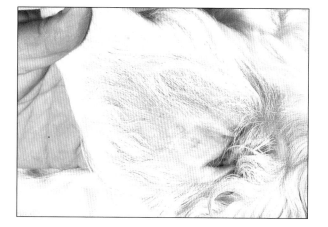

registered to you so that, if your lost dog turns up at a clinic or shelter, the chip can be scanned to retrieve your contact information.

The advantage of the microchip is that it is a permanent form of ID, but there are some factors to consider. Several different companies make microchips, and not all are compatible with the others' scanning devices. It's best to find a company with a universal microchip that can be read by scanners made by other companies as well. It won't do any good to have the dog chipped if the information cannot be retrieved. Also, not every humane society, shelter and clinic is equipped with a scanner, although more and more facilities are equipping themselves. In fact, many shelters microchip dogs that they adopt out to new homes.

Because the microchip is not visible to the eye, the dog must wear a tag that states that he is microchipped so that whoever picks him up will know to have him scanned. The microchip tag usually also lists the phone number of the registry and the dog's microchip number. He of course also should have a tag with your contact information in case his information cannot be retrieved. Humane societies and veterinary clinics offer microchipping service, which is usually very affordable.

Though less popular than microchipping, tattooing is another

permanent method of ID for dogs. Most vets perform this service, and there are also clinics that perform dog tattooing. This is also an affordable procedure and one that will not cause much discomfort for the dog. It is best to put the tattoo in a visible area, such as the ear, to deter theft. It is sad to say that there are cases of dogs' being stolen and sold to research laboratories, but such laboratories will not accept tattooed dogs.

To ensure that the tattoo is effective in aiding your dog's return to you, the tattoo number must be registered with a national organization. That way, when someone finds a tattooed dog, a phone call to the registry will quickly match the dog with his owner.

No dog should ever be without his identification tags, which should be securely attached to his everyday collar.

KUVASZ

BASIC TRAINING PRINCIPLES: PUPPY VS. ADULT

There's a big difference between training an adult dog and training a young puppy. With a young puppy, everything is new! At eight to ten weeks of age, he will be experiencing many things, and he has nothing with which to compare these experiences. Up to this point, he has been with his dam and litter-mates, not one-on-one with people except in his interactions with his breeder and visitors to the litter.

Life with a well-trained Kuvasz is mutually rewarding.

When you first bring the puppy home, he is eager to please you. This means that he accepts doing things your way. During the next couple of months, he will absorb the basis of everything he needs to know for the rest of his life. This early age is even referred to as the "sponge" stage. After that, for the next 18 months, it's up to you to reinforce good manners by building on the foundation that you've established early on. Once your puppy is reliable in basic commands and behavior and has reached the appropriate age, you may gradually introduce him to some of the interesting sports, games and activities available to pet owners and their dogs.

Raising your Kuvasz puppy is a family affair so that he respects and responds to everyone in the household. Each member of the family must know what rules to set forth for the puppy and how to use the same one-word commands to mean exactly the same thing every time. While the puppy should learn to obey commands from everyone in the family, one person will soon be considered by the pup to be the leader, the alpha person in his pack, the "boss" who must be obeyed. Often that highly regarded person turns out to be the one who feeds the puppy. Food ranks very high on the puppy's list of important things! That's why your puppy is rewarded with small treats along with verbal praise when he responds to you correctly. As the puppy learns to do what you want him to do, the food rewards are gradually eliminated and only the praise remains. If you were to keep up with the food treats, you could have two problems on your hands—an obese dog and a beggar.

OUR CANINE KIDS

"Everything I learned about parenting, I learned from my dog." How often adults recognize that their parenting skills are mere extensions of the education they acquired while caring for their dogs. Many owners refer to their dogs as their "kids" and treat their canine companions like real members of the family. Surveys indicate that a majority of dog owners talk to their dogs regularly, celebrate their dogs' birthdays and purchase Christmas gifts for their dogs. Another survey shows that dog owners take their dogs to the veterinarian more frequently than they visit their own physicians.

Your puppy looks to you for love, care, safety, guidance and discipline.

Training begins the minute your Kuvasz puppy steps through the doorway of your home, so don't make the mistake of putting the puppy on the floor and telling him by your actions to "Go for it! Run wild!" Even if this is your first puppy, you must act as if you know what you're doing: be the boss. A Kuvasz pup is more than ready to step into the leadership role if you do not. Before you collected your puppy, you decided where his own special place would be, and that's where to put him when you first arrive home. Give him a house tour after he has investigated his area and had a nap and a bathroom "pit stop."

It's worth mentioning here that if you've adopted an adult dog that is completely trained to your liking, lucky you! You're off the hook! However, if that dog spent his life up to this point in a home or living situation where he did not receive the proper training, be prepared to tackle the job ahead. A dog three years of age or older with no previous training cannot be blamed for not knowing what he was never taught. While the dog is trying to understand and learn your rules, at the same time he has to unlearn many of his previously self-taught habits and general view of the world.

Working with a professional trainer who knows the Kuvasz will speed up your progress with an adopted adult dog. You'll need patience, too. Some new rules may be close to impossible for the dog to accept. After all, he's been successful so far by doing everything his way. (Patience again.) He may agree with your instruction for a few days and then slip back into his old ways, so you must be just as consistent and understanding in your

teaching as you would be with a puppy. (More patience needed yet again!) Your dog has to learn to pay attention to your voice, your family, the daily routine, new smells, new sounds and, in some cases, even a new climate.

One of the most important things to find out about a newly adopted adult dog is his reaction to children (yours and others), strangers and your friends, and how he acts upon meeting other dogs. If he was not socialized with dogs as a puppy, this could be a major problem. This does not mean that he's a "bad" dog, a vicious dog or an aggressive dog; rather, it means that he has no idea how to read another dog's body language. There's no way for him to tell whether the other dog is a friend or foe. Survival instinct

Train your Kuvasz to always use the same area of property for bathroom duties. This makes for more convenient toileting as well as clean up.

takes over, telling him to attack first and ask questions later. This definitely calls for professional help and, even then, may not be a behavior that can be corrected 100% reliably (or even at all). If you have a Kuvasz puppy, this is why it is so very important to introduce your young puppy properly to other puppies and "dog-friendly" adult dogs. We have mentioned socialization many times to emphasize its importance.

HOUSE-TRAINING YOUR KUVASZ

Dogs are tactility-oriented when it comes to house-training. In other words, they respond to the surface on which they are given approval to eliminate. The choice is yours (the dog's version is in parentheses): The lawn (including the neighbors' lawns)? A bare patch of earth under a tree (where people like to sit and relax in the summertime)? Concrete steps or patio (all sidewalks, garages and basement floors)? The curbside (watch out for cars)? A small area of crushed stone in a corner of the yard (mine!)? The latter is the best choice if you can manage it, because it will remain strictly for the dog's use and is easy to keep clean.

You can start out with paper-training a young puppy indoors and switch over to an outdoor surface as the puppy matures and

DAILY SCHEDULE
How many relief trips does your puppy need per day? A puppy up to the age of 14 weeks will need to go outside about 8 to 12 times per day! You will have to take the pup out any time he starts sniffing around the floor or turning in small circles, as well as after naps, meals, games and lessons or whenever he's released from his crate. Once the puppy is 14 to 22 weeks of age, he will require only 6 to 8 relief trips. At the ages of 22 to 32 weeks, the puppy will require about 5 to 7 trips. Adult dogs typically require 4 relief trips per day, in the morning, afternoon, evening and late at night.

gains control over his need to eliminate. For the naysayers, don't worry—this won't mean that the dog will soil on every piece of newspaper lying around the house. You are training him to go outside, remember? Starting out by paper-training often is the only choice for a city dog.

WHEN YOUR PUPPY'S "GOT TO GO"

Your puppy's need to relieve himself is seemingly non-stop, but signs of improvement will be seen each week. From 8 to 10 weeks old, the puppy will have to be taken outside every time he wakes up, about 10–15 minutes after every meal and after every period of play—all day long, from first

A wire ex-pen is a helpful tool for providing your pup with an area of safe confinement.

thing in the morning until his bedtime. That's a total of ten or more trips per day to teach the puppy where it's okay to relieve himself. With that schedule in mind, you can see that house-training a young puppy is not a part-time job. It requires someone to be home all day.

If that seems overwhelming or impossible, do a little planning. For example, plan to pick up your puppy at the start of a vacation period. If you can't get home in the middle of the day, plan to hire a dog-sitter or ask a neighbor to come over to take the pup outside, feed him his lunch and then take him out again about ten or so minutes after he's eaten. Also make arrangements with that or another person to be your "emergency" contact if you have to stay late on the job. Remind yourself—repeatedly—that this hectic schedule improves as the puppy gets older.

A wire crate is fine for inside your home. The puppy gets a full view of what's going on around him while being safely confined in his own private den.

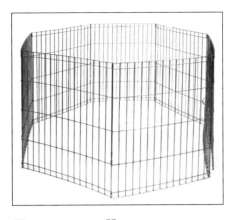

HOME WITHIN A HOME

Your Kuvasz puppy needs to be confined to one secure, puppy-proof area when no one is able to watch his every move. Generally the kitchen is the place of choice because the floor is washable. Likewise, it's a busy family area that will accustom the pup to a variety of noises, everything from pots and pans to the telephone, blender and dishwasher. He will also be enchanted by the smell of your cooking (and will never be critical when you burn something). A sturdy exercise pen (also called an "ex-pen," a puppy version of a playpen), with high enough sides to contain the pup, within the room of choice is an excellent means of confinement for a young pup. He can see out and has a certain amount of space in which to run about, but he is safe from dangerous things like electrical cords, heating units, trash baskets or open kitchen-supply cabinets. Place the pen where the puppy will not get a blast of heat or air conditioning.

In the pen, you can put a few toys, his bed (which can be his crate if the dimensions of pen and crate are compatible) and a few layers of newspaper in one small corner, just in case. A water bowl can be hung at a convenient height on the side of the ex-pen so it won't become a splashing pool for an innovative puppy. His food dish can go on the floor, next to (not under) the water bowl.

Crates are something that pet owners are at last getting used to for their dogs. Wild or domestic canines have always preferred to sleep in den-like safe spots, and that is exactly what the crate provides. How often have you seen adult dogs that choose to sleep under a table or chair even though they have full run of the house? It's the den connection. Crates are a huge help in house-training, as dogs instinctively do not want to soil their dens.

In your "happy" voice, use the word "Crate" every time you put the pup into his den. If he's new to a crate, toss in a small biscuit for him to chase the first few times. At night, after he's been outside, he should sleep in his crate. The crate may be kept in his designated area at night or, if you want to be sure to hear those wake-up yips in the morning, put the crate in a corner of your bedroom. However, don't make

BASIC PRINCIPLES OF DOG TRAINING

1. Start training early. A young puppy is ready, willing and able.
2. Timing is your all-important tool. Praise at the exact time that the dog responds correctly. Pay close attention.
3. Patience is almost as important as timing!
4. Repeat! The same word has to mean the same thing every time.
5. In the beginning, praise all correct behavior verbally, along with treats and petting.

Most dogs sniff around before they relieve themselves. Given the high sensitivity of dogs' noses—estimated at a million times the sensitivity of the human nose—owners may never comprehend the importance of this ritual.

any response whatsoever to whining or crying. If he's completely ignored, he'll settle down and get to sleep.

Good bedding for a young puppy is an old folded bath towel or an old blanket, something that is easily washable and disposable if necessary ("accidents" will happen!). Never put newspaper in the puppy's crate. Also, those old ideas about adding a clock to replace his mother's heartbeat, or a hot-water bottle to replace her warmth, are just that—old ideas. The clock could drive the puppy nuts, and the hot-water bottle could end up as a very soggy waterbed! An extremely good breeder would have introduced your puppy to the crate by letting two pups sleep together for a

couple of nights, followed by several nights alone. How thankful you will be if you found that breeder!

Safe toys in the pup's crate or area will keep him occupied, but monitor their condition closely. Discard any toys that show signs of being chewed to bits. Squeaky parts, bits of stuffing or plastic or any other small pieces can cause intestinal blockage or possibly choking if swallowed.

PROGRESSING WITH POTTY-TRAINING
After you've taken your puppy out and he has relieved himself in the area you've selected, he can have some free time with the family as long as there is someone responsible for watching him. That doesn't mean just someone

TIME TO PLAY!

Playtime can happen both indoors and out. A young puppy is growing so rapidly that he needs sleep more than he needs a lot of physical exercise. Puppies get sufficient exercise on their own just through normal puppy activity. Monitor play with young children so you can remove the puppy when he's had enough, or calm the kids if they get too rowdy. Almost all puppies love to chase after a toy you've thrown, and you can turn your games into educational activities. Every time your puppy brings the toy back to you, say "Give it" (or "Drop it") followed by "Good dog" and throwing it again. If he's reluctant to give it to you, offer a small treat so that he drops the toy as he takes the treat. He will soon get the idea.

position, which is something entirely different.

Most corrections at this stage come in the form of simply distracting the puppy. Instead of telling him "No" for "Don't chew the carpet," distract the chomping puppy with a toy and he'll forget about the carpet.

As you are playing with the pup, do not forget to watch him closely and pay attention to his body language. Whenever you see him begin to circle or sniff, take the puppy outside to relieve himself. If you are paper-training, put him back into his confined area on the newspapers. In either case, praise him as he eliminates while he actually is in the act of

in the same room who is watching TV or busy on the computer but one person who is doing nothing other than keeping an eye on the pup, playing with him on the floor and helping him understand his position in the pack.

This first taste of freedom will let you begin to set the house rules. If you don't want the dog on the furniture, now is the time to prevent his first attempts to jump up onto the couch. The word to use in this case is "Off," not "Down." "Down" is the word you will use to teach the down

Even dogs who live in outside enclosures need to be taken out for potty time so their homes remain clean.

Be consistent in
potty training
your Kuvasz and
he quickly will
move to the head
of the class.

relieving himself. Three seconds after he has finished is too late. You'll be praising him for running toward you, picking up a toy or whatever he may be doing at that moment, and that's not what you want to be praising him for. Timing is a vital tool in all dog training. Use it.

Remove soiled newspapers immediately and replace them with clean ones. You may want to take a small piece of soiled paper and place it in the middle of the new clean papers, as the scent will attract him to that spot when it's time to go again. That scent attraction is why it's so important to clean up any messes made in the house by using a product specially made to eliminate the odor of dog urine and droppings. Regular household cleansers won't do the trick. Pet shops sell the best pet deodorizers. Invest in the largest container you can find.

Scent attraction eventually will lead your pup to his chosen spot outdoors; this is the basis of outdoor training. When you take your puppy outside to relieve himself, use a one-word command such as "Outside" or "Go-potty" (that's one word to the puppy!) as you attach his leash. Then lead him to his spot. Now comes the hard part—hard for you, that is. Just stand there until he urinates and defecates. Move him a few feet in one direction or another if he's just sitting there looking at you, but remember that this is neither playtime nor time for a walk. This is strictly a business trip! Then, as he circles and squats (remember your timing!), give him a quiet "Good dog" as praise. If you start to jump for joy, ecstatic over his performance, he'll do one of two things: either he will stop mid-stream, as it were, or he'll do it again for you— in the house—and expect you to be just as delighted!

Give him five minutes or so and, if he doesn't go in that time, take him back indoors to his confined area and try again in another ten minutes or immediately if you see him sniffing and circling. By careful observation, you'll soon work out a successful schedule.

Accidents, by the way, are just that—accidents. Clean them up quickly and thoroughly, without comment, after the puppy has been taken outside to finish his business and then put back into his area or crate. If you witness an accident in progress, say "No!" in a stern voice and get the pup outdoors immediately. No punishment is needed. You and your puppy are just learning each other's language, and sometimes it's easy to miss a puppy's message. Chalk it up to experience and watch more closely from now on.

KEEPING THE PACK ORDERLY

Discipline is a form of training that brings order to life. For example, military discipline is what allows the soldiers in an army to work as one. Discipline is a form of teaching and, in dogs, is the basis of how the successful pack operates. Each member knows his place in the pack and all respect the leader, or alpha dog. It is essential for your puppy that you establish this type of relationship, with you as the alpha, or leader. It is a form of social coexistence that all canines recognize and accept. Discipline, therefore, is never to be confused with punishment. When you teach your puppy how you want him to behave, and he behaves properly and you praise him for it, you are disciplining him with a form of positive reinforcement. This is the type of training that works best with Kuvaszok, who do not respond well to negative training methods.

As the pack leader, it is up to you to keep an eye on your charge's whereabouts, especially when he is outdoors, blending in with the snow.

For a dog, rewards come in the form of praise, a smile, a cheerful tone of voice, a few friendly pats or a rub of the ears. Rewards are also small food treats. Obviously, that does not mean bits of regular dog food. Instead, treats are very small bits of special things like cheese or pieces of soft dog treats. The idea is to reward the dog with something very small that he can taste and swallow, providing

Be patient when training in a safely enclosed outdoor location, as there are plenty of distractions that will vie for your dog's attention.

instant positive reinforcement. If he has to take time to chew the treat, by the time he is finished he will have forgotten what he did to earn it.

Your puppy should never be physically punished. The displeasure shown on your face and in your voice is sufficient to signal to the pup that he has done something wrong. He wants to please everyone higher up on the social ladder, especially his leader, so a scowl and harsh voice will take care of the error. Growling out the word "Shame!" when the pup is caught in the act of doing something wrong is better than the repetitive "No." Some dogs hear "No" so often that they begin to think it's their name! By the way, do not use the dog's name when you're correcting him. His name is reserved to get his attention for something pleasant about to take place.

There are punishments that have nothing to do with you. For example, your dog may think that chasing cats is one reason for his existence. You can try to stop it as much as you like but without success, because it's such fun for the dog. But one good hissing, spitting swipe of a cat's claws across the dog's nose will put an end to the game forever. Intervene only when your dog's eyeball is seriously at risk. Cat scratches can cause permanent damage to an innocent but annoying puppy.

PUPPY KINDERGARTEN

Collar and Leash

Before you begin your Kuvasz puppy's education, he must be used to his collar and leash. Choose a collar for your puppy that is secure but not heavy or bulky. He won't enjoy training if he's uncomfortable. A flat buckle collar is fine for everyday wear and for initial puppy training. For older dogs, there are several types of training collars such as the martingale, which is a double loop that tightens slightly around the neck, or the head collar, which is similar to a horse's halter. A chain choke collar is not recommended for Kuvaszok, as it can pull and damage the abundant coat.

A lightweight 6-foot woven cotton or nylon training leash is preferred by most trainers because it is easy to fold up in your hand and comfortable to hold because there is a certain amount of give to it. There are lessons where the dog will start off 6 feet away from you at the end of the leash. The leash used to take the puppy outside to relieve himself is shorter because you don't want him to roam away from his area. The shorter leash will also be the one to use when you walk the puppy.

If you've been wise enough to enroll in a puppy kindergarten training class, suggestions will be

All training should take place with your Kuvasz on lead. Only attempt off-lead training in a securely fenced area.

made as to the best collar and leash for your young puppy. I say "wise" because your puppy will be in a class with puppies in his age range (up to five months old) of all breeds and sizes. It's the perfect way for him to learn the right way (and the wrong way) to interact with other dogs as well as their people. You cannot teach your puppy how to interpret another dog's sign language. For a Kuvasz owner, these socialization classes are invaluable. For novice and experienced dog owners alike, they are a real boon to further training.

Attention

You've been using the dog's name since the minute you collected him from the breeder, so you should be able to get his attention by saying his name—with a big smile and in an excited tone of voice. His response will be the puppy equivalent of "Here I am! What are we going to do?" Your immediate response (if you haven't guessed by now) is "Good dog." Rewarding him at the moment he pays attention to you teaches him the proper way to respond when he hears his name.

EXERCISES FOR A BASIC CANINE EDUCATION

THE SIT EXERCISE
There are several ways to teach the puppy to sit. The first one is to catch him whenever he is about to sit and, as his backside nears the floor, say "Sit, good dog!" That's positive reinforcement and, if your timing is sharp, he will learn that what he's doing at that second is connected to your

In teaching the sit exercise, you may have to begin by guiding your dog into the sit position until he gets the idea.

> **SIT AROUND THE HOUSE**
> "Sit" is the command you'll use most often. Your pup objects when placed in a sit with your hands, so try the "bringing the food up under his chin" method. Better still, catch him in the act! Your dog will sit on his own many times throughout the day, so let him know that he's doing the "Sit" by rewarding him. Praise him and have him sit for everything—toys, connecting his leash, his dinner, before going out the door, etc.

saying "Sit" and that you think he's clever for doing it.

Another method is to start with the puppy on his leash in front of you. Show him a treat in the palm of your right hand. Bring your hand up under his nose and, almost in slow motion, move your hand up and back so his nose goes up in the air and his head tilts back as he follows the treat in your hand. At that point, he will have to either sit or fall over, so as his back legs buckle under, say "Sit, good dog," and then give him the treat and lots of praise. You may have to begin with your hand lightly running up his chest, actually lifting his chin up until he sits. Some (usually older) dogs require gentle pressure on their hindquarters with the left hand, in which case the dog should be on your left side. Puppies generally do not appreciate this physical dominance.

After a few times, you should be able to show the dog a treat in the open palm of your hand, raise your hand waist-high as you say "Sit" and have him sit. You thereby will have taught him two things at the same time. Both the verbal command and the motion of the hand are signals for the sit. Your puppy is watching you almost more than he is listening to you, so what you do is just as important as what you say.

Don't save any of these drills only for training sessions. Use them as much as possible at odd times during a normal day to practice and to reinforce your role as leader. The dog should always sit before being given his food dish. He should sit to let you go through a doorway first, when the doorbell rings or when you stop to speak to someone on the street.

THE DOWN EXERCISE

Before beginning to teach the down command, you must consider how the dog feels about this exercise. To him, "down" is a submissive position. Being flat on the floor with you standing over him is not his idea of fun. It's up to you to let him know that, while it may not be fun, the reward of your approval is worth his effort.

Start with the puppy on your left side in a sit position. Hold the leash right above his collar in your left hand. Have an extra-special treat, such as a small piece of cooked chicken or hot dog, in your right hand. Place it at the end of the pup's nose and steadily move your hand down and forward along the ground. Hold

Use treats wisely in training. Hold the treats up to get the pup's attention, then reward him when he executes the command properly.

Most dogs will flop into the down position on their own with no problem but are more resistant when commanded into the down.

the leash to prevent a sudden lunge for the food. As the puppy goes into the down position, say "Down" very gently.

The difficulty with this exercise is twofold: it's both the submissive aspect and the fact that most people say the word "Down" as if they were drill sergeants in charge of recruits! So

DOWN

"Down" is a harsh-sounding word and a submissive posture in dog body language, thus presenting two obstacles in teaching the down command. When the dog is about to flop down on his own, tell him "Good down." Pups that are not good about being handled learn better by having food lowered in front of them. A dog that trusts you can be gently guided into position. When you give the command "Down," be sure to say it sweetly!

issue the command sweetly, give him the treat and have the pup maintain the down position for several seconds. If he tries to get up immediately, place your hands on his shoulders and press down gently, giving him a very quiet "Good dog." As you progress with this lesson, increase the "down time" until he will hold it until you say "Okay" (his cue for release). Practice this one in the house at various times throughout the day.

By increasing the length of time during which the dog must maintain the down position, you'll find many uses for it. For example, he can lie at your feet in the vet's office or anywhere that both of you have to wait, when you are on the phone, while the family is eating and so forth. If you progress to training for competitive obedience, he'll already be all set for the exercise called the "long down."

THE STAY EXERCISE
You can teach your Kuvasz to stay in the sit, down and stand positions. To teach the sit/stay, have the dog sit on your left side. Hold the leash at waist level in your left hand and let the dog know that you have a treat in your closed right hand. Step forward on your right foot as you say "Stay." Immediately turn and stand directly in front of the dog, keeping your right hand up high

so he'll keep his eye on the treat hand and maintain the sit position for a count of five. Return to your original position and offer the reward.

Increase the length of the sit/stay each time until the dog can hold it for at least 30 seconds without moving. After about a week of success, move out on your right foot and take two steps before turning to face the dog. Give the "Stay" hand signal (left palm back toward the dog's head) as you leave. He gets the treat when you return and he holds the sit/stay. Increase the distance that you walk away from him before turning until you reach the length of your training leash. But don't rush it! Go back to the beginning if he moves before he should. No matter what the lesson, never be upset by having to back up for a few days. The repetition and practice are what will make your dog reliable in these commands. It won't do any good to move on to something more difficult if the command is not mastered at the easier levels. Above all, even if you do get frustrated, never let your puppy know. Always keep a positive, upbeat attitude during training, which will transmit to your dog for positive results.

The down/stay is taught in the same way once the dog is completely reliable and steady with the down command. Again,

don't rush it. With the dog in the down position on your left side, step out on your right foot as you say "Stay." Return by walking around in back of the dog and into your original position. While you are training, it's okay to murmur something like "Hold on" to encourage him to stay put. When the dog will stay without moving when you are at a distance of 3 or 4 feet, begin to increase the length of time before you return. Be sure he holds the down on your return until you say "Okay." At that point, he gets his treat—just so he'll remember for next time that it's not over until it's over.

You want your Kuvasz to come running enthusiastically when he hears you call him.

COME AND GET IT!

The come command is your dog's safety signal. Until he is 99% perfect in responding, don't use the come command if you cannot enforce it. Practice on leash with treats or squeakers, or whenever the dog is running to you. Never call him to come to you if he is to be corrected for a misdemeanor. Reward the dog with a treat and happy praise whenever he comes to you.

THE COME EXERCISE

No command is more important to the safety of your Kuvasz than "Come." It is what you should say every single time you see the puppy running toward you: "Willie, come! Good dog." During playtime, run a few feet away from the puppy and turn and tell him to "Come" as he is already running to you. You can go so far as to teach your puppy two things

at once if you squat down and hold out your arms. As the pup gets close to you and you're saying "Good dog," bring your right arm in about waist high. Now he's also learning the hand signal, an excellent device should you be on the phone when you need to get him to come to you! You'll also both be one step ahead when you enter obedience classes.

When the puppy responds to your well-timed "Come," try it with the puppy on the training leash. This time, catch him off guard, while he's sniffing a leaf or watching a bird: "Willie, come!" You may have to pause for a split second after his name to be sure you have his attention. If the puppy shows any sign of confusion, give the leash a mild jerk and take a couple of steps backward. Do not repeat the command. In this case, you should say "Good come" as he reaches you.

That's the number-one rule of training. Each command word is given just once. Anything more is nagging. You'll also notice that all commands are one word only. Even when they are actually two words, you say them as one.

Never call the dog to come to you—with or without his name— if you are angry or intend to correct him for some misbehavior. When correcting the pup, you go to him. Your dog must always connect "Come" with something pleasant and with your approval; then you can rely on his response.

Puppies, like children, have notoriously short attention spans, so don't overdo it with any of the training. Keep each lesson short. Break it up with a quick run around the yard or a ball toss, repeat the lesson and quit as soon as the pup gets it right. That way, you will always end with a "Good dog."

Life isn't perfect and neither are puppies. A time will come, often around ten months of age, when he'll become "selectively deaf" or choose to "forget" his name. He may respond by wagging his tail (and even seeming to smile at you) with a look that says "Make me!" Laugh, throw his favorite toy and skip the lesson you had planned. Pups will be pups!

THE HEEL EXERCISE

The second most important command to teach, after the come, is the heel. When you are walking your growing puppy, you need to be in control. Besides, it looks

With a dog as strong as the Kuvasz, teaching your dog to behave properly on lead is essential.

terrible to bc pulled and yanked down the street, and it's not much fun either. Your eight- to ten-week-old puppy will probably follow you everywhere, but that's his natural instinct, not your control over the situation. However, any time he does follow you, you can say "Heel" and be ahead of the game, as he will learn to associate this command with the action of following you before you even begin teaching him to heel.

There is a very precise, almost military, procedure for teaching your dog to heel. As with all other obedience training, begin with the dog on your left side. He will be in a very nice sit and you will have

Be persistent in heel training your Kuvasz. It may take time before your dog is successful at following this command, but it is essential to ensure proper behavior and safety.

the training leash across your chest. Hold the loop and folded leash in your right hand. Pick up the slack leash above the dog in your left hand and hold it loosely at your side. Step out on your left foot as you say "Heel." If the puppy does not move, give a gentle tug or pat your left leg to get him started. If he surges ahead of you, stop and pull him back gently until he is at your side. Tell him to sit and begin again.

Walk a few steps and stop while the puppy is correctly beside you. Tell him to sit and give mild verbal praise. (More enthusiastic praise will encourage him to think the lesson is over.) Repeat the lesson, increasing the number of steps you take only as long as the dog is heeling nicely beside you. When you end the lesson, have him hold the sit, then give him the "Okay" to let him know that this is the end of the lesson. Praise him so that he knows he did a good job.

The cure for excessive pulling (a common problem) is to stop when the dog is no more than 2 or 3 feet ahead of you. Guide him back into position and begin again. With a really determined puller, try switching to a head collar. This will automatically turn the pup's head toward you so you can bring him back easily to the heel position. Give quiet, reassuring praise every time the leash goes slack and he's staying with you.

If your dog gets too far ahead of you when heel training, stop and bring him back into proper position before trying again.

Staying and heeling can take a lot out of a dog, so provide playtime and free-running exercise to shake off the stress when the lessons are over. You don't want him to associate training with all work and no fun.

TAPERING OFF TIDBITS
Your dog has been watching you—and the hand that treats—throughout all of his lessons, and now it's time to break the treat habit. Begin by giving him treats at the end of each lesson only. Then start to give a treat after the end of only some of the lessons. At the end of every lesson, as well as during the lessons, be consistent with the praise. Your pup now doesn't know whether he'll get a treat or not, but he should keep performing well just in case. Finally, you will stop giving treat rewards entirely. Save them for something brand-new that you want to teach him. Keep up the praise and you'll always have a "good dog."

OBEDIENCE CLASSES

The advantages of an obedience class are that your dog will have to learn amid the distractions of other people and dogs and that your mistakes will be quickly corrected by the trainer. Teaching your dog along with a qualified instructor and other handlers who may have more dog experience than you is another plus of the class environment. The instructor and other handlers can help you to find the most efficient way of teaching your dog a command or exercise. It's often easier to learn from other people's mistakes than your own. You will also learn all of the requirements for competitive obedience trials, in which you can earn titles and go on to advanced jumping and retrieving exercises, which are fun for many dogs. Obedience classes build the foundation needed for many other canine activities (in which we humans are allowed to participate, too!).

TRAINING FOR OTHER ACTIVITIES

Once your dog has basic obedience under his collar and is at least 12 months of age, you can enter the world of agility training. Dogs think agility is pure fun, like being turned loose in an amusement park full of obstacles! In addition to agility, tracking events that are open to all "nosey" dogs (which would include all dogs!). For those who like to volunteer, there is the wonderful feeling of owning a therapy dog and visiting hospices, nursing homes and veterans' homes to bring smiles, comfort and companionship to those who live there.

Around the house, your Kuvasz can be taught to do some simple chores. You might teach him to carry some small household items or to fetch the morning newspaper. The kids can teach the dog all kinds of tricks, from playing hide-and-seek to balancing a biscuit on his nose. A family dog is what rounds out the family. Everything he does, including lying at your feet and gazing lovingly at you, represents the bonus of owning a dog.

Your Kuvasz can be easily trained with food rewards. Most dogs live to eat, so food rewards can be very effective if not overused.

A well-trained Kuvasz is not only a joy to be around but can also be trained to participate in a number of doggie activities that will be fun for all.

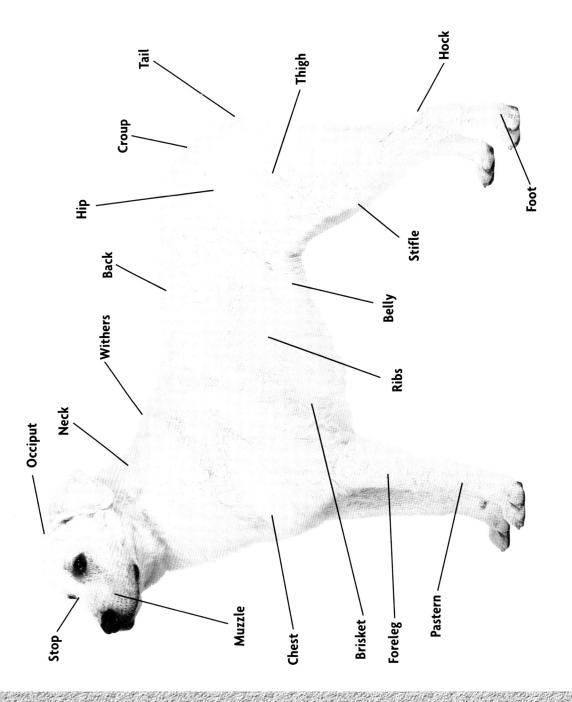

Tail

Croup

Hip

Back

Withers

Neck

Occiput

Stop

Muzzle

Chest

Brisket

Foreleg

Pastern

Ribs

Belly

Thigh

Stifle

Hock

Foot

PHYSICAL STRUCTURE OF THE KUVASZ

HEALTHCARE OF YOUR

KUVASZ

By Lowell Ackerman DVM, DACVD

HEALTHCARE FOR A LIFETIME

When you own a dog, you become his healthcare advocate over his entire lifespan, as well as being the one to shoulder the financial burden of such care. Accordingly, it is worthwhile to focus on prevention rather than treatment, as you and your pet will both be happier.

Of course, the best place to have begun your program of preventive healthcare is with the initial purchase or adoption of your dog. There is no way of guaranteeing that your new furry friend is free of medical problems, but there are some things you can do to improve your odds. You certainly should have done adequate research into the Kuvasz and have selected your puppy carefully rather than buying on impulse. Health issues aside, a large number of pet abandonment and relinquishment cases arise from a mismatch between pet needs and owner expectations. This is entirely preventable with appropriate planning and finding a good breeder.

Regarding healthcare issues specifically, it is very difficult to make blanket statements about where to acquire a problem-free pet, but, again, a reputable breeder is your best bet. In an ideal situation you have the opportunity to see both parents, get references from other owners of the breeder's pups and see genetic-testing documentation for several generations of the litter's ancestors. At the very least, you must thoroughly investigate the Kuvasz and the problems inherent in the breed, as well as the genetic testing available to screen for those problems. Genetic testing offers some important benefits but is available for only a few disorders in a relatively small number of breeds and is not available for some of the most common genetic diseases, such as hip dysplasia, cataracts, epilepsy, cardiomyopathy, etc. This area of research is indeed exciting and increasingly important, and advances will continue to be made each year. In fact, recent research has shown that there is an equivalent dog gene for 75% of known human genes, so research done in either species is likely to benefit the other.

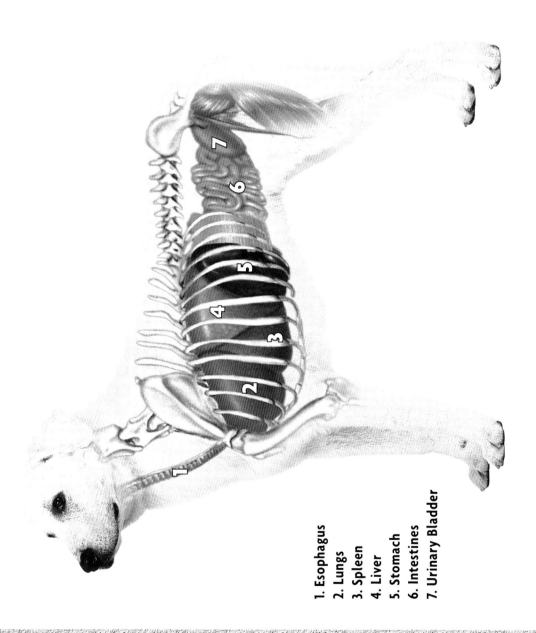

1. Esophagus
2. Lungs
3. Spleen
4. Liver
5. Stomach
6. Intestines
7. Urinary Bladder

INTERNAL ORGANS OF THE KUVASZ

We've also discussed that evaluating the behavioral nature of your Kuvasz and that of his immediate family members is an important part of the selection process that cannot be overemphasized. It is sometimes difficult to evaluate temperament in puppies because certain behavioral tendencies, such as some forms of aggression, may not be immediately evident. More dogs are euthanized each year for behavioral reasons than for all medical conditions combined, so it is critical to take temperament issues seriously. Start with a well-balanced, friendly companion and put the time and effort into proper socialization, and you will both be rewarded with a valued relationship for the life of the dog.

Assuming that you have started off with a pup from healthy, sound stock, you then become responsible for helping your veterinarian keep your pet healthy. Some crucial things happen before you even bring your puppy home. Parasite control typically begins at two weeks of age, and vaccinations typically begin at six to eight weeks of age. A pre-pubertal evaluation is typically scheduled for about six months of age. At this time, a dental evaluation is done (since the adult teeth are now in), heartworm prevention is started and neutering or spaying is most commonly done.

It is critical to commence regular dental care at home if you have not already done so. It may not sound very important, but most dogs have active periodontal disease by four years of age if they don't have their teeth cleaned regularly at home, not just at their veterinary exams. Dental problems lead to more than just bad "doggy breath." Gum disease can have very serious medical consequences. If you start brushing your dog's teeth and using antiseptic rinses from a young age, your dog will be accustomed to it and will not resist. The results will be healthy dentition, which your pet will need to enjoy a long, healthy life.

Many dogs are considered adults at a year of age, although some larger breeds like the Kuvasz continue filling out until two or so years old. Even individual dogs

DENTAL CONCERNS
A veterinary dental exam is necessary if you notice one or any combination of the following in your dog:
• Broken, loose or missing teeth
• Loss of appetite (which could be due to mouth pain or illness caused by infection)
• Gum abnormalities, including redness, swelling and bleeding
• Drooling, with or without blood
• Yellowing of the teeth or gumline, indicating tartar
• Bad breath

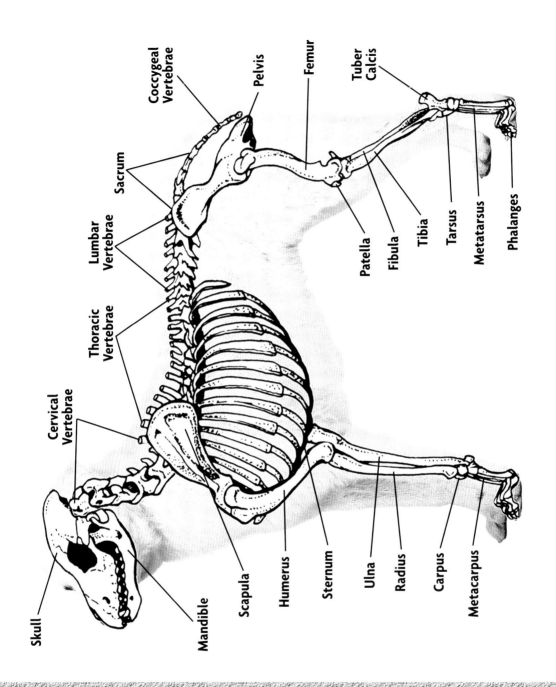

Coccygeal Vertebrae

Pelvis

Femur

Tuber Calcis

Sacrum

Lumbar Vertebrae

Thoracic Vertebrae

Patella

Fibula

Tibia

Tarsus

Metatarsus

Phalanges

Cervical Vertebrae

Skull

Mandible

Scapula

Humerus

Sternum

Ulna

Radius

Carpus

Metacarpus

Skeletal Structure of the Kuvasz

within each breed have different healthcare requirements, so work with your veterinarian to determine what will be needed and what your role should be. This doctor-client relationship is important, because as vaccination guidelines change, there may not be an annual "vaccine visit" scheduled. You must make sure that you see your veterinarian at least annually, even if no vaccines are due, because this is the best opportunity to coordinate healthcare activities and to make sure that no medical issues creep by unaddressed.

When your Kuvasz reaches three-quarters of his anticipated lifespan, he is considered a "senior" and will require some special care. In general, if you've been taking great care of your canine companion throughout his formative and adult years, the transition to senior status should be a smooth one. Age is not a disease, and as long as everything is functioning as it should, there is no reason why most of late adulthood should not be rewarding for both you and your pet. This is especially true if you have tended to the details, such as regular veterinary visits, proper dental care, excellent nutrition and management of bone and joint issues.

At this stage in your Kuvasz's life, your veterinarian should schedule visits twice yearly, instead of once, to run some laboratory screenings, electrocardiograms and the like, and to change the diet to something more digestible. Catching problems early is the best way to manage them effectively. Treating the early stages of heart disease is so much easier than trying to intervene when there is more significant damage to the heart muscle. Similarly, managing the beginning of kidney problems is fairly routine if there is no significant kidney damage. Other problems, like cognitive dysfunction (similar to senility and Alzheimer's disease), cancer, diabetes and arthritis, are more common in older dogs, but all can be treated to help the dog live as many happy, comfortable years as possible. Just as in people, medical management is more effective (and less expensive) when you catch things early.

SELECTING A VETERINARIAN
There is probably no more important decision that you will make regarding your pet's healthcare than the selection of his doctor. Your pet's veterinarian will be a pediatrician, family-practice physician and gerontologist, depending on the dog's life stage, and will be the individual who makes recommendations regarding issues such as when specialists need to be consulted, when diagnostic testing and/or

therapeutic intervention is needed and when you will need to seek outside emergency and critical-care services. Your vet will act as your advocate and liaison throughout these processes.

Everyone has his own idea about what to look for in a vet, an individual who will play a big role in his dog's (and, of course, his own) life for many years to come. For some, it is the compassionate caregiver with whom they hope to develop a professional relation-

TAKING YOUR DOG'S TEMPERATURE

It is important to know how to take your dog's temperature at times when you think he may be ill. It's not the most enjoyable task, but it can be done without too much difficulty. It's easier with a helper, preferably someone with whom the dog is friendly, so that one of you can hold the dog while the other inserts the thermometer.

Before inserting the thermometer, coat the end with petroleum jelly. Insert the thermometer slowly and gently into the dog's rectum about one inch. Wait for the reading, about two minutes. Be sure to remove the thermometer carefully and clean it thoroughly after each use.

A dog's normal body temperature is between 100.5 and 102.5 degrees F. Immediate veterinary attention is required if the dog's temperature is below 99 or above 104 degrees F.

ship to span the lives of their dogs and even their future pets. For others, they are seeking a clinician with keen diagnostic and therapeutic insight who can deliver state-of-the-art healthcare. Still others need a veterinary facility that is open evenings and weekends, is in close proximity or provides mobile veterinary services, to accommodate their schedules; these people may not much mind that their dogs might see different veterinarians on each visit.

Just as we have different reasons for selecting our own healthcare professionals (e.g., covered by insurance plan, expert in field, convenient location, etc.), we should not expect that there is a one-size-fits-all recommendation for selecting a veterinarian and veterinary practice. The best advice is to be honest in your assessment of what you expect from a veterinary practice and to conscientiously research the options in your area. You will quickly appreciate that not all veterinary practices are the same, and you will be happiest with one that truly meets your needs. For your Kuvasz, you are wise to choose a vet who is knowledge-able about large breeds and who also is familiar with the Kuvasz and its specific issues, such as anesthesia sensitivity and possible reactions to certain drugs and vaccines.

There is another point to be considered in the selection of veterinary services. Not that long ago, a single veterinarian would attempt to manage all medical and surgical issues as they arose. That was often problematic, because veterinarians are trained in many species and many diseases, and it was just impossible for general veterinary practitioners to be experts in every species, every breed, every field and every ailment. However, just as in the human healthcare fields, specialization has allowed general practitioners to concentrate on primary healthcare delivery, especially wellness and the prevention of infectious diseases, and to utilize a network of specialists to assist in the management of conditions that require specific expertise and experience. Thus there are now many types of veterinary specialists, including dermatologists, cardiologists, ophthalmologists, surgeons, internists, oncologists, neurologists, behaviorists, criticalists and others to help primary-care veterinarians deal with complicated medical challenges. In most cases, specialists see cases referred by primary-care veterinarians, make diagnoses and set up management plans. From there, the animals' ongoing care is returned to their primary-care veterinarians. This important team approach to your pet's medical-care needs has provided opportu-

nities for advanced care and an unparalleled level of quality to be delivered.

With all of the opportunities for your Kuvasz to receive high-quality veterinary medical care, there is another topic that needs to be addressed at the same time—cost. It's been said that you can have excellent healthcare or inexpensive healthcare, but never both; this is as true in veterinary medicine as it is in human medicine. While veterinary costs are a fraction of what the same services cost in the human health-care arena, it is still difficult to deal with unanticipated medical costs, especially since they can easily creep into hundreds or even thousands of dollars if specialists or emergency services become involved. However, there are ways of managing these risks. The easiest is to buy pet health

Guarantee a better chance for your Kuvasz to live a long, healthy life by bringing him to the veterinarian soon after bringing him home and for regular follow-up visits.

COMMON INFECTIOUS DISEASES

Let's discuss some of the diseases that create the need for vaccination in the first place. Following are the major canine infectious diseases and a simple explanation of each.

Rabies: A devastating viral disease that can be fatal in dogs and people. In fact, vaccination of dogs and cats is an important public-health measure to create a resistant animal buffer population to protect people from contracting the disease. Vaccination schedules are determined on a government level and are not optional for pet owners; rabies vaccination is required by law in all 50 states.

Parvovirus: A severe, potentially life-threatening disease that is easily transmitted between dogs. There are four strains of the virus, but it is believed that there is significant "cross-protection" between strains that may be included in individual vaccines.

Distemper: A potentially severe and life-threatening disease with a relatively high risk of exposure, especially in certain regions. In very high-risk distemper environments, young pups may be vaccinated with human measles vaccine, a related virus that offers cross-protection when administered at four to ten weeks of age.

Hepatitis: Caused by canine adenovirus type 1 (CAV-1), but since vaccination with the causative virus has a higher rate of adverse effects, cross-protection is derived from the use of adenovirus type 2 (CAV-2), a cause of respiratory disease and one of the potential causes of canine cough. Vaccination with CAV-2 provides long-term immunity against hepatitis, but relatively less protection against respiratory infection.

Canine cough: Also called tracheobronchitis, actually a fairly complicated result of viral and bacterial offenders; therefore, even with vaccination, protection is incomplete. Wherever dogs congregate, canine cough will likely be spread among them. Intranasal vaccination with *Bordetella* and parainfluenza is the best safeguard, but the duration of immunity does not appear to be very long, typically a year at most. These are non-core vaccines, but vaccination is sometimes mandated by boarding kennels, obedience classes, dog shows and other places where dogs congregate to try to minimize spread of infection.

Leptospirosis: A potentially fatal disease that is more common in some geographic regions. It is capable of being spread to humans. The disease varies with the individual "serovar," or strain, of *Leptospira* involved. Since there does not appear to be much cross-protection between serovars, protection is only as good as the likelihood that the serovar in the vaccine is the same as the one in the pet's local environment. Problems with *Leptospira* vaccines are that protection does not last very long, side effects are not uncommon and a large percentage of dogs (perhaps 30%) may not respond to vaccination.

Borrelia burgdorferi: The cause of Lyme disease, the risk of which varies with the geographic area in which the pet lives and travels. Lyme disease is spread by deer ticks in the eastern US and western black-legged ticks in the western part of the country, and the risk of exposure is high in some regions. Lameness, fever and inappetence are most commonly seen in affected dogs. The extent of protection from the vaccine has not been conclusively demonstrated.

Coronavirus: This disease has a high risk of exposure, especially in areas where dogs congregate, but it typically causes only mild to moderate digestive upset (diarrhea, vomiting, etc.). Vaccines are available, but the duration of protection is believed to be relatively short and the effectiveness of the vaccine in preventing infection is considered low.

There are many other vaccinations available, including those for *Giardia* and canine adenovirus-1. While there may be some specific indications for their use, and local risk factors to be considered, they are not widely recommended for most dogs.

insurance and realize that its foremost purpose is not to cover routine healthcare visits but rather to serve as an umbrella for those rainy days when your pet needs medical care and you don't want to worry about whether or not you can afford that care.

Pet insurance policies are very cost-effective (and very inexpensive by human health-insurance standards), but make sure that you buy the policy long before you intend to use it (preferably starting in puppyhood, because coverage will exclude pre-existing conditions) and that you are actually buying an indemnity insurance plan from an insurance company that is regulated by your state or province. Many insurance policy look-alikes are actually discount clubs that are redeemable only at specific locations and for specific services. An indemnity plan covers your pet at almost all veterinary, specialty and emergency practices and is an excellent way to manage your pet's ongoing healthcare needs.

VACCINATIONS AND INFECTIOUS DISEASES

There has never been an easier time to prevent a variety of infectious diseases in your dog, but the advances we've made in veterinary medicine come with a price—choice. Now while it may seem that choice regarding your pet's vaccinations is a good thing

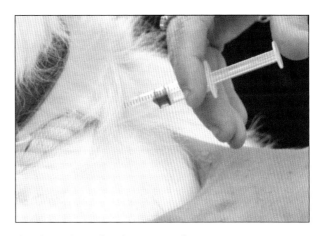

(and it is), it also has never been more difficult for the pet owner (or the veterinarian) to make an informed decision about the best way to protect pets through vaccination.

Years ago, it was just accepted that puppies got a starter series of vaccinations and then annual "boosters" throughout their lives to keep them protected. As more and more vaccines became available, consumers wanted the convenience of having all of that protection in a single injection. The result was "multivalent" vaccines that crammed a lot of protection into a single syringe. The manufacturers' recommendations were to give the vaccines annually, and this was a simple enough protocol to follow. However, as veterinary medicine has become more sophisticated and we have started looking more at healthcare quandaries rather than convenience, it became

Booster shots, when necessary, are one of the things you can expect at your Kuvasz's annual veterinary check-up.

necessary to reevaluate the situation and deal with some tough questions. It is important to realize that whether or not to use a particular vaccine depends on the risk of contracting the disease against which it protects, the severity of the disease if it is contracted, the duration of immunity provided by the vaccine, the safety of the product and the needs of the individual animal. In a very general sense, rabies, distemper, hepatitis and parvovirus are considered core vaccine needs, while parainfluenza, *Bordetella bronchiseptica*, leptospirosis, coronavirus and borreliosis (Lyme disease) are considered non-core needs and best reserved for animals that demonstrate reasonable risk of contracting the diseases.

NEUTERING/SPAYING
Sterilization procedures (neutering for males/spaying for females) are meant to accomplish several purposes. While the underlying premise is to address the risk of pet overpopulation, there are also some medical and behavioral benefits to the surgeries as well. For females, spaying prior to the first estrus (heat cycle) leads to a marked reduction in the risk of mammary cancer and other serious female problems. There also will be no manifestations of

"heat" to attract male dogs and no bleeding in the house. For males, there is prevention of testicular cancer and a reduction in the risk of prostate problems. In both sexes there may be some limited reduction in aggressive behaviors toward other dogs, and some diminishing of urine marking, roaming and mounting.

While neutering and spaying do indeed prevent animals from contributing to pet overpopulation, even no-cost and low-cost neutering options have not eliminated the problem. Perhaps one of the main reasons for this is that individuals that intentionally breed their dogs and those that allow their animals to run at large are the main causes of unwanted offspring. Also, animals in shelters are often there because they were abandoned or relinquished, not because they came from unplanned matings. Neutering/spaying is important, but it should be considered in the context of the real causes of animals' ending up in shelters and eventually being euthanized.

One of the important considerations regarding neutering is that it is a surgical procedure. This sometimes gets lost in discussions of low-cost procedures and commoditization of the process. In females, spaying is specifically referred to as an ovariohysterectomy. In this procedure, a midline incision is made in the abdomen and the entire uterus and both ovaries are surgically removed. While this is a major invasive surgical procedure, it usually has few complications, because it is typically performed on healthy young animals. However, it is major surgery, as any woman who has had a hysterectomy will attest.

In males, neutering has traditionally referred to castration, which involves the surgical removal of both testicles. While still a significant piece of surgery, there is not the abdominal exposure that is required in the female surgery. In addition, there is now a chemical sterilization option, in which a solution is injected into each testicle, leading to atrophy of the sperm-producing cells. This can typically be done under sedation rather than full anesthesia. This is a relatively new approach, and there are no long-term clinical studies yet available.

Neutering/spaying is typically done around six months of age at most veterinary hospitals, although techniques have been pioneered to perform the procedures in animals as young as eight weeks of age. In general, the surgeries on the very young animals are done for

---

SPAY'S THE WAY

Although spaying a female dog qualifies as major surgery—an ovariohysterectomy, in fact—this procedure is regarded as routine when performed by a qualified veterinarian on a healthy dog. The advantages to spaying a bitch are many and great. Spayed dogs do not develop uterine cancer or any life-threatening diseases of the genitals. Likewise, spayed dogs are at a significantly reduced risk of breast cancer. Bitches (and owners) are relieved of the demands of heat cycles. A spayed bitch will not leave bloody stains on your furniture during estrus, and you will not have to contend with single-minded macho males trying to climb your fence in order to seduce her. The spayed bitch's coat will not show the ill effects of her estrogen level's climbing such as a dull, lackluster outer coat or patches of hairlessness.

---

the specific reason of sterilizing them before they go to their new homes. This is done in some shelter hospitals for assurance that the animals will definitely not produce any pups. Otherwise, these organizations need to rely on owners to comply with their wishes to have the animals "altered" at a later date, something that does not always happen.

There are some exciting immunocontraceptive "vaccines" currently under development, and there may be a time when contraception in pets will not require surgical procedures. We anxiously await these developments.

A scanning electron micrograph of a dog flea, *Ctenocephalides canis*, on dog hair.

S. E. M. BY DR. DENNIS KUNKEL, UNIVERSITY OF HAWAII.

EXTERNAL PARASITES

FLEAS

Fleas have been around for millions of years and, while we have better tools now for controlling them than at any time in the past, there still is little chance that they will end up on an endangered species list. Actually, they are very well adapted to living on our pets, and they continue to adapt as we make advances.

The female flea can consume 15 times her weight in blood during active reproduction and can lay as many as 40 eggs a day. These eggs are very resistant to the effects of insecticides. They hatch into larvae, which then mature and spin cocoons. The immature fleas reside in this pupal stage until the time is right for feeding. This pupal stage is also very resistant to the effects of insecticides, and pupae can last in the environment without feeding for many months. Newly emergent fleas are attracted to animals by the warmth of the animals' bodies, movement and exhaled carbon dioxide. However, when they first emerge from their cocoons, they orient towards light; thus when an animal passes between a flea and the light source, casting a shadow, the flea pounces and starts to feed. If the animal turns out to be a dog or cat, the reproductive cycle continues. If the flea lands on another type of animal, including a

FLEA PREVENTION FOR YOUR DOG

- Discuss with your veterinarian the safest product to protect your dog, likely in the form of a monthly tablet or a liquid preparation placed on the back of the dog's neck.
- For dogs suffering from flea-bite dermatitis, a shampoo or topical insecticide treatment is required.
- Your lawn and property should be sprayed with an insecticide designed to kill fleas and ticks that lurk outdoors.
- Using a flea comb, check the dog's coat regularly for any signs of parasites.
- Practice good housekeeping. Vacuum floors, carpets and furniture regularly, especially in the areas that the dog frequents, and wash the dog's bedding weekly.
- Follow up house-cleaning with carpet shampoos and sprays to rid the house of fleas at all stages of development. Insect growth regulators are the safest option.

person, the flea will bite but will then look for a more appropriate host. An emerging adult flea can survive without feeding for up to 12 months but, once it tastes blood, it can survive off its host for only 3 to 4 days.

It was once thought that fleas spend most of their lives in the environment, but we now know that fleas won't willingly jump off a dog unless leaping to another dog or when physically removed by brushing, bathing or other manipulation. Flea eggs, on the other hand, are shiny and smooth, and they roll off the animal and into the environment. The eggs, larvae and pupae then exist in the environment, but once the adult finds a susceptible animal, it's home sweet home until the flea is forced to seek refuge elsewhere.

Since adult fleas live on the animal and immature forms survive in the environment, a successful treatment plan must address all stages of the flea life cycle. There are now several safe and effective flea-control products that can be applied on a monthly basis. These include fipronil, imidacloprid, selamectin and permethrin (found in several formulations). Most of these products have significant flea-killing rates within 24 hours. However, none of them will control the immature forms in the environment. To accomplish this, there are a variety of insect growth regulators that can be sprayed into the

THE FLEA'S LIFE CYCLE

What came first, the flea or the egg? This age-old mystery is more difficult to comprehend than the actual cycle of the flea. Fleas usually live only about four months. A female can lay 2,000 eggs in her lifetime.

PHOTO BY CAROLINA BIOLOGICAL SUPPLY CO.

Egg

After ten days of rolling around your carpet or under your furniture, the eggs hatch into larvae, which feed on various and sundry debris. In days or months, depending on the climate, the larvae spin cocoons and develop into the pupal or nymph stage, which quickly develop into fleas.

Larva

Pupa

These immature fleas must locate a host within 10 to 14 days or they will die. Only about 1% of the flea population exist as adult fleas, while the other 99% exist as eggs, larvae or pupae.

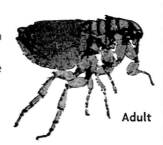

Adult

environment (e.g., pyriproxyfen, methoprene, fenoxycarb) as well as insect development inhibitors such as lufenuron that can be administered. These compounds have no effect on adult fleas, but they stop immature forms from developing into adults. In years gone by, we relied heavily on toxic insecticides (such as organophosphates, organochlorines and carbamates) to manage the flea problem, but today's options are not only much safer to use on our pets but also safer for the environment.

TICKS

Ticks are members of the spider class (arachnids) and are blood-sucking parasites capable of transmitting a variety of diseases, including Lyme disease, ehrlichiosis, babesiosis and Rocky Mountain spotted fever. It's easy to see ticks on your own skin, but it is more of a challenge when your furry companion is affected. Whenever you happen to be planning a stroll in a tick-infested area (especially forests, grassy or wooded areas or parks) be prepared to do a thorough inspection of your dog afterward to search for ticks. Ticks can be tricky,

> ### TICK CONTROL
> Removal of underbrush and leaf litter and the thinning of trees in areas where tick control is desired are recommended. These actions remove the cover and food sources for small animals that serve as hosts for ticks. With continued mowing of grasses in these areas, the probability of ticks' surviving is further reduced. A variety of insecticide ingredients (e.g., resmethrin, carbaryl, permethrin, chlorpyrifos, dioxathion and allethrin) are registered for tick control around the home.

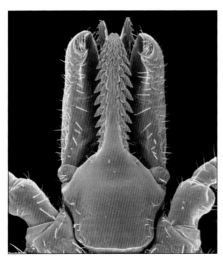

A scanning electron micrograph of the head of a female deer tick, *Ixodes dammini*, a parasitic tick that carries Lyme disease.

so make sure you spend time looking in the ears, between the toes and everywhere else where a tick might hide. Ticks need to be attached for 24–72 hours before they transmit most of the diseases that they carry, so you do have a window of opportunity for some preventive intervention.

Female ticks live to eat and breed. They can lay between 4,000 and 5,000 eggs and they die soon after. Males, on the other hand, live only to mate with the females and continue the process as long as they are able. Most ticks live on multiple hosts before parasitizing dogs. The immature forms typically reside on grass and shrubs, waiting for susceptible animals to walk by. The larvae and nymph stages typically feed on wildlife.

If only a few ticks are present on a dog, they can be plucked out, but it is important to remove the

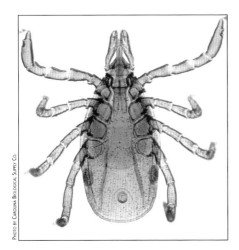

entire head and mouthparts, which may be deeply embedded in the skin. This is best accomplished with forceps designed especially for this purpose; fingers can be used but should be protected with rubber gloves, plastic wrap or at least a paper towel. The tick should be grasped as closely as possible to the animal's skin and should be pulled upward with steady, even pressure. Do not squeeze, crush or puncture the body of the tick or you risk exposure to any disease carried by that tick. Once the ticks have been removed, the sites of attachment should be disinfected. Your hands should then be washed with soap and water to further minimize risk of contagion. The tick should be disposed of in a container of alcohol or household bleach.

MITES

Mites are tiny arachnid parasites that parasitize the skin of dogs. Skin diseases caused by mites are referred to as "mange," and there are many different forms seen in dogs. These forms are very different from one another, each one warranting an individual description.

Sarcoptic mange, or scabies, is one of the itchiest conditions that affects dogs. The microscopic *Sarcoptes* mites burrow into the superficial layers of the skin and can drive dogs crazy with itchiness. They are also communicable to people, although they can't complete their reproductive cycle on people. In addition to being tiny, the mites also are often difficult to find when trying to make a diagnosis. Skin scrapings from multiple areas are examined microscopically but, even then, sometimes the mites cannot be found.

Deer tick, *Ixodes dammini.*

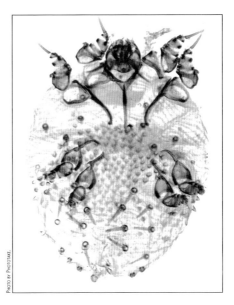

Sarcoptes scabiei, commonly known as the "itch mite."

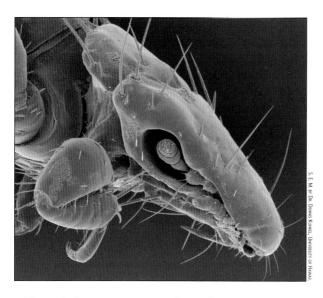

S.E.M. BY DR. DENNIS KUNKEL, UNIVERSITY OF HAWAII

Micrograph of a dog louse, *Heterodoxus spiniger*. Female lice attach their eggs to the hairs of the dog. As the eggs hatch, the larval lice bite and feed on the blood. Lice can also feed on dead skin and hair. This feeding activity can cause hair loss and skin problems.

Illustration of *Demodex folliculoram*.

Fortunately, scabies is relatively easy to treat, and there are a variety of products that will successfully kill the mites. Since the mites can't live in the environment for very long without feeding, a complete cure is usually possible within four to eight weeks.

Cheyletiellosis is caused by a relatively large mite, which sometimes can be seen even without a microscope. Often referred to as "walking dandruff," this also causes itching, but not usually as profound as with scabies. While *Cheyletiella* mites can survive somewhat longer in the environment than scabies mites, they too are relatively easy to treat, being responsive to not only the medications used to treat scabies but also often to flea-control products.

Otodectes cynotis is the canine ear mite and is one of the more common causes of mange, especially in young dogs in shelters or pet stores. That's because the mites are typically present in large numbers and are quickly spread to nearby animals. The mites rarely do much harm but can be difficult to eradicate if the treatment regimen is not comprehensive. While many try to treat the condition with ear drops only, this is the most common cause of treatment failure. Ear drops cause the mites to simply move out of the ears and as far away as possible (usually to the base of the tail) until the insecticide levels in the ears drop to an acceptable level—then it's back to business as usual! The successful treatment of ear mites requires treating all animals in the household with a systemic insecticide, such as selamectin, or a combination of miticidal ear drops combined with whole-body flea-control preparations.

Demodicosis, sometimes referred to as red mange, can be one of the most difficult forms of mange to treat. Part of the problem has to do with the fact that the mites live in the hair follicles and they are relatively well shielded from topical and systemic products. The main issue, however, is that demodectic mange typically results only when there is some underlying process interfering with the

ILLUSTRATION BY PHOTOTAKE

dog's immune system.

Since *Demodex* mites are normal residents of the skin of mammals, including humans, there is usually a mite population explosion only when the immune system fails to keep the number of mites in check. In young animals, the immune deficit may be transient or may reflect an actual inherited immune problem. In older animals, demodicosis is usually seen only when there is another disease hampering the immune system, such as diabetes, cancer, thyroid problems or the use of immune-suppressing drugs. Accordingly, treatment involves not only trying to kill the mange mites but also discerning what is interfering with immune function and correcting it if possible.

Chiggers represent several different species of mite that don't parasitize dogs specifically, but do latch on to passersby and can cause irritation. The problem is most prevalent in wooded areas in the late summer and fall. Treatment is not difficult, as the mites do not complete their life cycle on dogs and are susceptible to a variety of miticidal products.

MOSQUITOES

Mosquitoes have long been known to transmit a variety of diseases to people, as well as just being biting pests during warm weather. They also pose a real risk to pets. Not only do they carry deadly heart-worms but recently there also has been much concern over their involvement with West Nile virus. While we can avoid heartworm with the use of preventive medications, there are no such preventives for West Nile virus. The only method of prevention in endemic areas is active mosquito control. Fortunately, most dogs that have been exposed to the virus only developed flu-like symptoms and, to date, there have not been the large number of reported deaths in canines as seen in some other species.

MOSQUITO REPELLENT
Low concentrations of DEET (less than 10%), found in many human mosquito repellents, have been safely used in dogs but, in these concentrations, probably give only about two hours of protection. DEET may be safe in these small concentrations, but since it is not licensed for use on dogs, there is no research proving its safety for dogs. Products containing permethrin give the longest-lasting protection, perhaps two to four weeks. As DEET is not licensed for use on dogs, and both DEET and permethrin can be quite toxic to cats, appropriate care should be exercised. Other products, such as those containing oil of citronella, also have some mosquito-repellent activity, but typically have a relatively short duration of action.

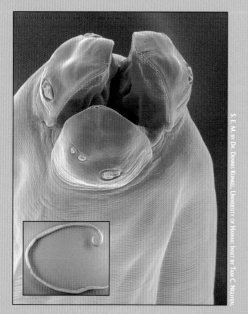

The ascarid roundworm *Toxocara canis,* showing the mouth with three lips. INSET: Photomicrograph of the roundworm *Ascaris lumbricoides.*

The hookworm *Ancylostoma caninum* infests the intestines of dogs. INSET: Note the row of teeth at the posterior end, used to anchor the worm to the intestinal wall.

INTERNAL PARASITES: WORMS

ASCARIDS

Ascarids are intestinal roundworms that rarely cause severe disease in dogs. Nonetheless, they are of major public health significance because they can be transferred to people. Sadly, it is children who are most commonly affected by the parasite, probably from inadvertently ingesting ascarid-contaminated soil. In fact, many yards and children's sandboxes contain appreciable numbers of ascarid eggs. So, while ascarids don't bite dogs or latch onto their intestines to suck blood, they do cause some nasty medical conditions in children and are best eradicated from our furry friends. Because pups can start passing ascarid eggs by three weeks of age, most parasite-control programs begin at two weeks of age and are repeated every two weeks until pups are eight weeks old. It is important to realize that bitches can pass ascarids to their pups even if they test negative prior to whelping. Accordingly, bitches are best treated at the same time as the pups.

HOOKWORMS

Unlike ascarids, hookworms do latch onto a dog's intestinal tract and can cause significant loss of blood and protein. Similar to ascarids, hookworms can be transmitted to humans, where they cause a condition known as cutaneous larval migrans. Dogs can become infected either by consuming the infective larvae or by the larvae's penetrating the skin directly. People most often get infected when they are lying on the ground (such as on a beach) and the larvae penetrate the skin. Yes, the larvae can penetrate through a beach blanket. Hookworms are typically susceptible to the same medications used to treat ascarids.

HEARTWORMS

Heartworm disease is caused by the parasite *Dirofilaria immitis* and is seen in dogs around the world. A member of the roundworm group, it is spread between dogs by the bite of an infected mosquito. The

WORM-CONTROL GUIDELINES

- Practice sanitary habits with your dog and home.
- Clean up after your dog and don't let him sniff or eat other dogs' droppings.
- Control insects and fleas in the dog's environment. Fleas, lice, cockroaches, beetles, mice and rats can act as hosts for various worms.
- Prevent dogs from eating uncooked meat, raw poultry and dead animals.
- Keep dogs and children from playing in sand and soil.
- Kennel dogs on cement or gravel; avoid dirt runs.
- Administer heartworm preventives regularly.
- Have your vet examine your dog's stools at your annual visits.
- Select a boarding kennel carefully so as to avoid contamination from other dogs or an unsanitary environment.
- Prevent dogs from roaming. Obey local leash laws.

PHOTO BY CAROLINA BIOLOGICAL SUPPLY CO.

Ascarid *Rhabditis*

PHOTO BY CAROLINA BIOLOGICAL SUPPLY CO.

Hookworm *Ancylostoma caninum*

PHOTO BY TAM C. NGUYEN.

Tapeworm *Dipylidium caninum*

PHOTO BY TAM C. NGUYEN.

Heartworm *Dirofilaria immitis*

mosquito injects infective larvae into the dog's skin with its bite, and these larvae develop under the skin for a period of time before making their way to the heart. There they develop into adults, which grow and create blockages of the heart, lungs and major blood vessels there. They also start producing offspring (microfilariae), and these microfilariae circulate in the bloodstream, waiting to hitch a ride when the next mosquito bites. Once in the mosquito, the microfilariae develop into infective larvae and the entire process is repeated.

When dogs get infected with heartworm, over time they tend

to develop symptoms associated with heart disease, such as coughing, exercise intolerance and potentially many other manifestations. Diagnosis is confirmed by either seeing the microfilariae themselves in blood samples or using immunologic tests (antigen testing) to identify the presence of adult heartworms. Since antigen tests measure the presence of adult heartworms and microfilarial tests measure offspring produced by adults, neither are positive until six to seven months after the initial infection. However, the beginning of damage can occur by fifth-stage larvae as early as three months after infection. Thus it is possible for dogs to be harboring problem-causing larvae for up to three months before either type of test would identify an infection.

The good news is that there are great protocols available for preventing heartworm in dogs. Testing is critical in the process, and it is important to understand the benefits as well as the limitations of such testing. All dogs six months of age or older that have not been on continuous heartworm-preventive medication should be screened with microfilarial or antigen tests. For dogs receiving preventive medication, periodic antigen testing helps assess the

The dog tapeworm *Taenia pisiformis*.

S. E. M. by Dr. Dennis Kunkel, University of Hawaii

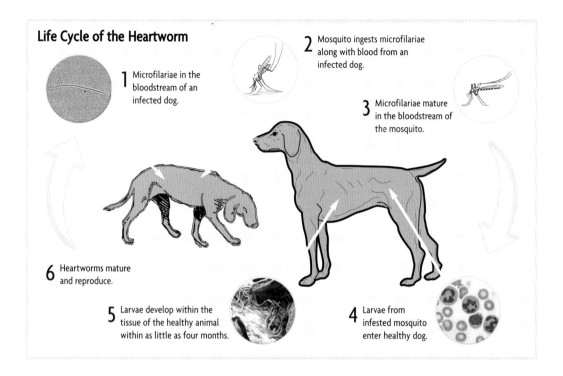

Life Cycle of the Heartworm

1 Microfilariae in the bloodstream of an infected dog.

2 Mosquito ingests microfilariae along with blood from an infected dog.

3 Microfilariae mature in the bloodstream of the mosquito.

6 Heartworms mature and reproduce.

5 Larvae develop within the tissue of the healthy animal within as little as four months.

4 Larvae from infested mosquito enter healthy dog.

effectiveness of the preventives. The American Heartworm Society guidelines suggest that annual retesting may not be necessary when owners have absolutely provided continuous heartworm prevention. Retesting on a two- to three-year interval may be sufficient in these cases. However, your veterinarian will likely have specific guidelines under which heartworm preventives will be prescribed, and many prefer to err on the side of safety and usually retest annually.

It is indeed fortunate that heartworm is relatively easy to prevent, because treatments can be as life-threatening as the disease itself. Treatment requires a two-step process that kills the adult heartworms first and then the microfilariae. Prevention is obviously preferable; this involves a once-monthly oral or topical treatment. The most common oral preventives include ivermectin (not suitable for some breeds), moxidectin and milbemycin oxime; the once-a-month topical drug selamectin provides heartworm protection in addition to flea, tick and other parasite controls.

SHOWING YOUR

KUVASZ

Is dog showing in your blood? Are you excited by the idea of gaiting your handsome Kuvasz around the ring to the thunderous applause of an enthusiastic audience? Are you certain that your beloved Kuvasz is flawless? You are not alone! Every loving owner thinks that his dog has no faults, or too few to mention. No matter how many times an owner reads the breed standard, he cannot find any faults in his aristocratic companion dog. If this sounds like you, and if you are considering entering your Kuvasz in a dog show, here are some basic questions to ask yourself:

- Did you purchase a "show-quality" puppy from the breeder?
- Is your puppy at least six months of age?
- Does the puppy exhibit correct show type for his breed?
- Does your puppy have any disqualifying faults?
- Is your Kuvasz registered with the American Kennel Club?

An accomplished handler in the making! Show dogs must be so well heel-trained that even a child can gait them (though such interactions must be supervised by an adult).

- How much time do you have to devote to training, grooming, conditioning and exhibiting your dog?
- Do you understand the rules and regulations of a dog show?
- Do you have time to learn how to show your dog properly?
- Do you have the financial resources to invest in showing your dog?
- Will you show the dog yourself or hire a professional handler?
- Do you have a vehicle that can accommodate your weekend trips to the dog shows?

Success in the show ring requires more than a pretty face, a wagging tail and a pocketful of liver. Even though dog shows can be exciting and enjoyable, the sport of conformation makes great demands on the exhibitors and the dogs. Winning exhibitors live for their dogs, devoting time and money to their dogs' presentation, conditioning and training. Very few novices, even those with good dogs, will find themselves in the winners' circle, though it does happen. Don't be disheartened, though. Every exhibitor began as a novice and worked his way up to the Group ring. It's the "working your way up" part that you must keep in mind.

Assuming that you have purchased a puppy of the correct type and quality for showing, let's begin to examine the world

FOR MORE INFORMATION...
For reliable, up-to-date information about registration, dog shows and other canine competitions, contact one of the national registries by mail or via the Internet.
American Kennel Club
5580 Centerview Dr., Raleigh, NC 27606-3390
www.akc.org

United Kennel Club
100 E. Kilgore Road, Kalamazoo, MI 49002
www.ukcdogs.com

Canadian Kennel Club
89 Skyway Ave., Suite 100, Etobicoke, Ontario
M9W 6R4, Canada
www.ckc.ca

The Kennel Club
1-5 Clarges St., Piccadilly,
London W1Y 8AB, UK
www.the-kennel-club.org.uk

of showing and what's required to get started. Although the entry fee into a dog show is nominal, there are lots of other hidden costs involved with "finishing" your Kuvasz, that is, making him a champion. Things like equipment, travel, training and conditioning all cost money. A more serious campaign will include fees for a professional handler, boarding, cross-country travel and advertising. Top-winning show dogs can represent a very considerable investment—over $100,000 has been spent in campaigning some dogs. (The investment can be less, of course,

MEETING THE IDEAL

The American Kennel Club defines a standard as: "A description of the ideal dog of each recognized breed, to serve as an ideal against which dogs are judged at shows." This "blueprint" is drawn up by the breed's recognized parent club, approved by a majority of its membership and then submitted to the AKC for approval. This is a complete departure from the way standards are handled in the UK, where all standards and changes are controlled by The Kennel Club.

    The AKC states that "An understanding of any breed must begin with its standard. This applies to all dogs, not just those intended for showing." The picture that the standard draws of the dog's type, gait, temperament and structure is the guiding image used by breeders as they plan their programs.

for owners who don't use professional handlers.)

Many owners, on the other hand, enter their "average" Kuvaszs in dog shows for the fun and enjoyment of it. Dog showing makes an absorbing hobby, with many rewards for dogs and owners alike. If you're having fun, meeting other people who share your interests and enjoying the overall experience, you likely will catch the "bug." Once the dog-show bug bites, its effects can last a lifetime; it's certainly much better than a deer tick! Soon you will be envisioning yourself in the center ring at the Westminster Kennel Club Dog Show in New York City, competing for the prestigious Best in Show cup. This magical dog show is televised annually from Madison Square Garden, and the victorious dog becomes a celebrity overnight.

AKC CONFORMATION SHOWING

GETTING STARTED

Visiting a dog show as a spectator is a great place to start. Pick up the show catalog to find out what time your breed is being shown, who is judging the breed and in which ring the classes will be held. To start, Kuvaszok compete against other Kuvaszok, and the winner is selected as Best of Breed by the judge. This is the procedure for each breed. At a group show, all of the Best of Breed winners go on to compete for Group One in their respective groups. For example, all Best of Breed winners in a given group compete against each other; this is done for all seven groups. Finally, all seven group winners go head to head in the ring for the Best in Show award.

What most spectators don't

understand is the basic idea of conformation. A dog show is often referred as a "conformation" show. This means that the judge should decide how each dog stacks up (conforms) to the breed standard for his given breed: how well does this Kuvasz conform to the ideal representative detailed in the standard? Ideally, this is what happens. In reality, however, this ideal often gets slighted as the judge compares Kuvasz #1 to Kuvasz #2. Again, the ideal is that each dog is judged based on his merits in comparison to his breed standard, not in comparison to the other dogs in the ring. It is easier for judges to compare dogs of the same breed to decide which they think is the better specimen; in the Group and Best in Show ring, however, it is very difficult to compare one breed to another, like apples to oranges. Thus the dog's conformation to the breed standard—not to mention advertising dollars and good handling—is essential to success in conformation shows. The dog described in the standard (the standard for each AKC breed is written and approved by the breed's national parent club and then submitted to the AKC for approval) is the perfect dog of that breed, and breeders keep their eye on the standard when they choose which dogs to breed, hoping to

get closer and closer to the ideal with each litter.

Another good first step for the novice is to join a dog club. You will be astonished by the many and different kinds of dog clubs in the country, with about 5,000 clubs holding events every year. Most clubs require that prospective new members present two letters of recommendation from existing members. Perhaps you've made some friends visiting a show held by a particular club and you would like to join that club. Dog clubs may specialize in a single breed, like a local or regional Kuvasz club, or in a specific pursuit, such as obedience, tracking or agility.

Ch. Ajándác Branco A Pazdasáe Ról at a show in Amsterdam in 2001.

Group 4

AKC-Eukanuba

December 12, 2001

Ch. Double Ring Moonlight Serenade placing in the Group at the prestigious AKC/Eukanuba Classic Invitational.

There are all-breed clubs for all dog enthusiasts; they sponsor special training days, seminars on topics like grooming or handling or lectures on breeding or canine genetics. There are also clubs that specialize in certain types of dogs, like working dogs, herding dogs, companion dogs, etc.

A parent club is the national organization, sanctioned by the AKC, which promotes and safe-guards its breed in the country. The Kuvasz Club of America was formed in 1966 and can be contacted on the Internet at

AKC GROUPS

For showing purposes, the American Kennel Club divides its recognized breeds into seven groups: Working Dogs, Hounds, Sporting Dogs, Terriers, Toys, Non-Sporting Dogs and Herding Dogs.

www.kuvasz.com. The parent club holds an annual national specialty show, usually in a different city each year, in which many of the country's top dogs, handlers and breeders gather to compete. At a specialty show, only members of a single breed are invited to participate. There are also group specialties, in which all members of a group are invited. For more information about dog clubs in your area, contact the AKC at www.akc.org on the Internet or write them at their Raleigh, NC address.

HOW SHOWS ARE ORGANIZED

Three kinds of conformation shows are offered by the AKC. There is the all-breed show, in which all AKC-recognized breeds can compete; the specialty show, which is for one breed only and usually sponsored by the breed's parent club and the group show, for all breeds in one of the AKC's seven groups. The Kuvasz competes in the Working Group.

For a dog to become an AKC champion of record, the dog must earn 15 points at shows. The points must be awarded by at least three different judges and must include two "majors" under different judges. A "major" is a three-, four- or five-point win, and the number of points per win is determined by the number of dogs competing in the show on that day. (Dogs that are absent or are excused are not counted.) The number of points that are awarded varies from breed to breed. More dogs are needed to attain a major in more popular breeds, and fewer dogs are

At a benched show, a dog remains in a designated area, when not competing, where visitors can meet him. These shows are rare in the US.

OAKLAND COUNTY
KENNEL CLUB

Ch. Glacier Creek's Artic Spirit takes a Best in Show at the Oakland County Kennel Club.

thcy are champions. Dogs that are not champions (referred to as "class dogs") compete in one of five classes. The class in which a dog is entered depends on age and previous show wins. First there is the Puppy Class (sometimes divided further into classes for 6- to 9-month-olds and 9- to 12-month-olds); next is the Novice Class (for dogs that have no points toward their championship and whose only first-place wins have come in the Puppy Class or the Novice Class, the latter class limited to three first places); then there is the

needed in less popular breeds. Yearly, the AKC evaluates the number of dogs in competition in each division (there are 14 divisions in all, based on geography) and may or may not change the numbers of dogs required for each number of points. For example, a major in Division 2 (Delaware, New Jersey and Pennsylvania) recently required 17 dogs or 16 bitches for a three-point major, 29 dogs or 27 bitches for a four-point major and 51 dogs or 46 bitches for a five-point major. The Kuvasz attracts numerically proportionate representation at all-breed shows.

Only one dog and one bitch of each breed can win points at a given show. There are no "co-ed" classes except for champions of record. Dogs and bitches do not compete against each other until

MEET THE AKC
The American Kennel Club is the main governing body of the dog sport in the United States. Founded in 1884, the AKC consists of 500 or more independent dog clubs plus 4,500 affiliated clubs, all of which follow the AKC rules and regulations. Additionally, the AKC maintains a registry for pure-bred dogs in the US and works to preserve the integrity of the sport and its continuation in the country. Over 1,000,000 dogs are registered each year, representing about 150 recognized breeds. There are over 15,000 competitive events held annually for which over 2,000,000 dogs enter to participate. Dogs compete to earn over 40 different titles, from champion to Companion Dog to Master Agility Champion.

American-bred Class (for dogs bred in the US); the Bred-by-Exhibitor Class (for dogs handled by their breeders or by immediate family members of their breeders); and the Open Class (for any non-champions). Any dog may enter the Open Class, regardless of age or win history, but to be competitive the dog should be older and have ring experience.

The judge at the show begins judging the male dogs in the Puppy Class(es) and proceeds through the other classes. The judge awards first through fourth place in each class. The first-place winners of each class then compete with one another in the Winners Class to determine Winners Dog. The judge then starts over with the bitches, beginning with the Puppy Class(es) and proceeding up to the Winners Class to award Winners Bitch, just as he did with the dogs. A Reserve Winners Dog and Reserve Winners Bitch are also selected; they could be awarded the points in the case of a disqualification.

The Winners Dog and Winners Bitch are the two that are awarded the points for their breed. They then go on to compete with any champions of record (often called "specials") of their breed that are entered in the show. The champions may be dogs or bitches; in this class, all are shown together. The judge reviews the Winners Dog and

Ch. Mauna-Ederra's Double Image won a Group placement at Westminster Kennel Club in 2001, a unique achievement for the breed.

Winners Bitch along with all of the champions to select the Best of Breed winner. The Best of Winners is selected between the Winners Dog and Winners Bitch; if one of these two is selected Best of Breed as well, he or she is automatically determined Best of Winners. Lastly, the judge selects Best of Opposite Sex to the Best of Breed winner. The Best of Breed winner then goes on to the group competition.

At a group or all-breed show, the Best of Breed winners from each breed are divided into their respective groups to compete against one another for Group One through Group Four. Group One (first place) is awarded to the dog that best lives up to the ideal for his breed as described in the standard. A group judge, therefore, must have a thorough working knowledge of many breed standards. After placements have been made in each group, the seven Group One winners (from the Working Group, Toy Group, Hound Group, etc.) compete against each other for the top honor, Best in Show.

There are different ways to find out about dog shows in your area. The American Kennel Club's monthly magazine, the *American Kennel Gazette*, is accompanied by the *Events Calendar*; this magazine is available through subscription. You can also look on the AKC's and your parent club's websites for information and check the event listings in your local newspaper.

Your Kuvasz must be six months of age or older and registered with the AKC in order to

Each dog's gait is evaluated in the show ring so that the judge can assess structure and movement.

Conformation shows can be rewarding experiences for both you and your dog.

be entered in AKC-sanctioned shows in which there are classes for the Kuvasz. Your Kuvasz also must not possess any disqualifying faults and must be sexually intact. The reason for the latter is simple: dog shows are the proving grounds to determine which dogs and bitches are worthy of being bred. If they cannot be bred, that defeats the purpose! On that note, only dogs that have achieved championships, thus proving their excellent quality, should be bred. If you have spayed or neutered your dog, however, there are many AKC events other than conformation, such as obedience trials, agility trials and the Canine Good Citizen® Program, in which you and your Kuvasz can participate.

OTHER TYPES OF COMPETITION

In addition to conformation shows, the AKC holds a variety of other competitive events. Obedience trials, agility trials and tracking trials are open to all breeds, while hunting tests, field trials, lure coursing, herding tests and trials, earthdog tests and coonhound events are limited to specific breeds or groups of breeds. The Junior Showmanship program is offered to aspiring young handlers and their dogs, and the Canine Good Citizen® Program is an all-around good-behavior test open to all dogs, purebred and mixed.

OBEDIENCE TRIALS

Mrs. Helen Whitehouse Walker, a Standard Poodle fancier, can be credited with introducing obedience trials to the United States. In the 1930s she designed a series of exercises based on those of the Associated Sheep, Police, Army Dog Society of Great Britain. These exercises were intended to evaluate the working relationship between dog and owner. Since those early days of the sport in the US, obedience trials have grown more and more popular, and now more than 2,000 trials each year attract over 100,000 dogs and their owners. Any dog registered with the AKC, regardless of neutering or other disqualifications that would preclude entry in conformation competition, can participate in obedience trials.

There are three levels of difficulty in obedience competition. The first (and easiest) level is the Novice, in which dogs can earn the Companion Dog (CD) title. The intermediate level is the Open level, in which the Companion Dog Excellent (CDX) title is awarded. The advanced level is the Utility level, in which dogs compete for the Utility Dog (UD) title. Classes at each level are further divided into "A" and "B," with "A" for beginners and "B" for those with more experience. In order to win a title at a given level, a dog must earn three "legs." A "leg" is accomplished when a dog scores 170 or higher (200 is a perfect score). The scoring system gets a little trickier when you understand that a dog must score more than 50% of the

Kuvaszok and their handlers get together for team obedience at the 2003 national specialty.

points available for each exercise in order to actually earn the points. Available points for each exercise range between 20 and 40.

A dog must complete different exercises at each level of obedience. The Novice exercises are the easiest, with the Open and finally the Utility levels progressing in difficulty. Examples of Novice exercises are on- and off-lead heeling, a figure-8 pattern, performing a recall (or come), long sit and long down and standing for examination. In the Open level, the Novice-level exercises are required again, but this time without a leash and for longer durations. In addition, the dog must clear a broad jump, retrieve over a jump and drop on recall. In the Utility level, the exercises are quite difficult, including executing basic commands based on hand signals, following a complex heeling pattern, locating articles based on scent discrimination and completing jumps at the handler's direction.

Once he's earned the UD title, a dog can go on to win the prestigious title of Utility Dog Excellent (UDX) by winning "legs" in ten shows. Additionally, Utility Dogs who win "legs" in Open B and Utility B earn points toward the lofty title of Obedience Trial Champion (OTCh.). Established in 1977 by the AKC, this title requires a dog to earn 100 points

JUNIOR SHOWMANSHIP

For budding dog handlers, ages 10 to 18 years, Junior Showmanship competitions are an excellent training ground for the next generation of dog professionals. Owning and caring for a dog are wonderful methods of teaching children responsibility, and Junior Showmanship builds upon that foundation. Juniors learn by grooming, handling and training their dogs, and the quality of a junior's presentation of the dog (and himself) is evaluated by a licensed judge. The junior can enter with any registered AKC dog to compete, including an Indefinite Listing Privilege, provided that the dog lives with him or a member of his family.

Junior Showmanship competitions are divided into two classes: Novice (for beginners) and Open (for juniors who have three first place wins in the Novice Class). The junior must run with the dog with the rest of the handlers and dogs, stack the dog for examination and individually gait the dog in a specific pattern. Juniors should practice with a handling class or an experienced handler before entering the Novice Class so that they recognize all the jargon that the judge may use.

A National Junior Organization was founded in 1997 to help promote the sport of dog showing among young people. The AKC also offers a Junior Scholarship for juniors who excel in the program.

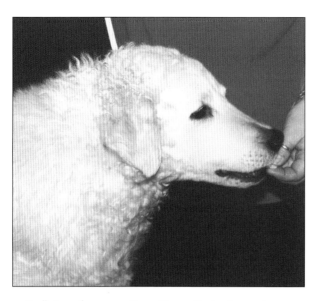

Small pieces of liver are often used as food rewards in the ring.

as well as three first places in a combination of Open B and Utility B classes under three different judges. The "brass ring" of obedience competition is the AKC's National Obedience Invitational. This is an exclusive competition for only the cream of the obedience crop. In order to qualify for the invitational, a dog must be ranked in either the top 25 all-breeds in obedience or in the top 3 for his breed in obedience. The title at stake here is that of National Obedience Champion (NOC).

AGILITY TRIALS

Agility trials became sanctioned by the AKC in August 1994, when the first licensed agility trials were held. Since that time, agility certainly has grown in popularity by leaps and bounds, literally! The AKC allows all registered breeds (including Miscellaneous Class breeds) to participate, providing the dog is 12 months of age or older. Agility is designed so that the handler demonstrates how well the dog can work at his side. The handler directs his dog through, over, under and around an obstacle course that includes jumps, tires, the dog walk, weave poles, pipe tunnels, collapsed tunnels and more. While working his way through the course, the dog must keep one eye and ear on the handler and the rest of his body on the course. The handler runs along with the dog, giving verbal and hand signals to guide the dog through the course.

The first organization to promote agility trials in the US was the United States Dog Agility Association, Inc. (USDAA). Established in 1986, the USDAA sparked the formation of many member clubs around the country. To participate in USDAA trials, dogs must be at least 18 months of age.

The USDAA and AKC both offer titles to winning dogs, although the exercises and requirements of the two organizations differ. Agility Dog (AD), Advanced Agility Dog (AAD) and Master Agility Dog (MAD) are the titles offered by the USDAA, while the AKC offers Novice Agility (NA), Open Agility (OA),

Agility Excellent (AX) and Master Agility Excellent (MX). Beyond these four AKC titles, dogs can win additional titles in "jumper" classes: Jumper with Weave Novice (NAJ), Open (OAJ) and Excellent (MXJ). The ultimate title in AKC agility is MACH, Master Agility Champion. Dogs can continue to add number designations to the MACH title, indicating how many times the dog has met the title's requirements (MACH1, MACH2 and so on).

Agility trials are a great way to keep your dog active, and they will keep you running, too! You should join a local agility club to learn more about the sport. These

It is quite a sight seeing this large guardian moving through an agility course with grace and determination.

clubs offer sessions in which you can introduce your dog to the various obstacles as well as training classes to prepare him for competition. In no time, your dog will be climbing A-frames, crossing the dog walk and flying over hurdles, all with you right beside him. Your heart will leap every time your dog jumps through the hoop—and you'll be having just as much (if not more) fun!

TRACKING

Tracking tests are exciting ways to test your Kuvasz's instinctive scenting ability on a competitive level. All dogs have a nose, and all breeds are welcome in tracking tests. The first AKC-licensed tracking test took place in 1937 as part of the Utility level at an obedience trial, and thus competitive tracking was officially begun. The first title, Tracking Dog (TD), was offered in 1947, ten years after the first official tracking test. It was not until 1980 that the American Kennel Club added the title Tracking Dog Excellent (TDX), which was followed by the title Variable Surface Tracking (VST) in 1995. Champion Tracker (CT) is awarded to a dog who has earned all three of those titles.

The TD level is the first and

most basic level in tracking, progressing in difficulty to the TDX and then the VST. A dog must follow a track laid by a human 30 to 120 minutes prior in order to earn the TD title. The track is about 500 yards long and contains up to 5 directional changes. At the next level, the TDX, the dog must follow a 3- to 5-hour-old track over a course that is up to 1,000 yards long and has up to 7 directional changes. In the most difficult level, the Variable Surface Tracking (VST), the track is up to 5 hours old and located in an urban setting.

Ch. Szumeria's Jamaican Music or "Marley," of course, wins Best of Breed at the prestigious Westminster Kennel Club Dog Show in 2003.

BEST OF BREED

THE
WESTMINSTER
KENNEL CLUB

INDEX

*Page numbers in **boldface** indicate illustrations.*

My Kuvasz

PUT YOUR PUPPY'S FIRST PICTURE HERE

Dog's Name _____

Date _____ Photographer _____